Professor: **Nikkel**   Course: **REL 1080**

Contents

Professor: **Nikkel**   Course: **REL 1080**

Contents

Faith and the Need for Evidence

Reason and Revelation

CHAPTER III.   ON THE WAY IN WHICH DIVINE TRUTH IS TO BE MADE KNOWN

(1) The way of making truth known is not always the same, and, as the Philosopher
has very well said, "it belongs to an educated man to seek such certitude in each thing
as the nature of that thing allows."[1] The remark is also introduced by Boethius.[2]
But, since such is the case, we must first show what way is open to us in order that
we may make known the truth which is our object.

(2) There is a twofold mode of truth in what we profess about God. Some truths
about God exceed all the ability of the human reason. Such is the truth that God is tri-
une. But there are some truths which the natural reason also is able to reach. Such are
that God exists, that He is one, and the like. In fact, such truths about God have been
proved demonstratively by the philosophers, guided by the light of the natural reason.

(3) That there are certain truths about God that totally surpass man's ability appears with the greatest evidence. Since, indeed, the principle of all knowledge that
the reason perceives about some thing is the understanding of the very substance of
that being (for according to Aristotle "what a thing is" is the principle of demonstration),[3] it is necessary that the way in which we understand the substance of a
thing determines the way in which we know what belongs to it. Hence, if the human
intellect comprehends the substance of some thing, for example, that of a stone or of
a triangle, no intelligible characteristic belonging to that thing surpasses the grasp of
the human reason. But this does not happen to us in the case of God. For the human
intellect is not able to reach a comprehension of the divine substance through its natural power. For, according to its manner of knowing in the present life, the intellect depends on the senses for the origin of knowledge; and so those things that
do not fall under the senses cannot be grasped by the human intellect except in

REASON AND REVELATION   From *On the Truth of the Catholic Faith: Summa Contra Gentiles,* Book I,
by St. Thomas Aquinas, translated by Anton C. Pegis. Copyright © 1955 by Doubleday, a division of
Bantam, Doubleday, Dell Publishing Group, Inc. Used by permission of Doubleday, a division of Bantam, Doubleday, Dell Publishing Group, Inc.

[1] Aristotle, *Nicomachean Ethics,* I, 3 (1094b 24).

[2] Boethius, *De Trinitate,* II, (PL, 64, col. 1250).

[3] Aristotle, *Posterior Analytics,* II, 3 (90b 31).

436

so far as the knowledge of them is gathered from sensible things. Now, sensible things cannot lead the human intellect to the point of seeing in them the nature of the divine substance; for sensible things are effects that fall short of the power of their cause. Yet, beginning with sensible things, our intellect is led to the point of knowing about God that He exists, and other such characteristics that must be attributed to the First Principle. There are, consequently, some intelligible truths about God that are open to the human reason; but there are others that absolutely surpass its power.

(4) We may easily see the same point from the gradation of intellects. Consider the case of two persons of whom one has a more penetrating grasp of a thing by his intellect than does the other. He who has the superior intellect understands many things that the other cannot grasp at all. Such is the case with a very simple person who cannot at all grasp the subtle speculations of philosophy. But the intellect of an angel surpasses the human intellect much more than the intellect of the greatest philosopher surpasses the intellect of the most uncultivated simple person; for the distance between the best philosopher and a simple person is contained within the limits of the human species, which the angelic intellect surpasses. For the angel knows God on the basis of a more noble effect than does man; and this by as much as the substance of an angel, through which the angel in his natural knowledge is led to the knowledge of God, is nobler than sensible things and even than the soul itself, through which the human intellect mounts to the knowledge of God. The divine intellect surpasses the angelic intellect much more than the angelic surpasses the human. For the divine intellect is in its capacity equal to its substance, and therefore it understands fully what it is, including all its intelligible attributes. But by his natural knowledge the angel does not know what God is, since the substance itself of the angel, through which he is led to the knowledge of God, is an effect that is not equal to the power of its cause. Hence, the angel is not able, by means of his natural knowledge, to grasp all the things that God understands in Himself; nor is the human reason sufficient to grasp all the things that the angel understands through his own natural power. Just as, therefore, it would be the height of folly for a simple person to assert that what a philosopher proposes is false on the ground that he himself cannot understand it, so (and even more so) it is the acme of stupidity for a man to suspect as false what is divinely revealed through the ministry of the angels simply because it cannot be investigated by reason.

(5) The same thing, moreover, appears quite clearly from the defect that we experience every day in our knowledge of things. We do not know a great many of the properties of sensible things, and in most cases we are not able to discover fully the natures of those properties that we apprehend by the sense. Much more is it the case, therefore, that the human reason is not equal to the task of investigating all the intelligible characteristics of that most excellent substance.

(6) The remark of Aristotle likewise agrees with this conclusion. He says that "our intellect is related to the prime beings, which are most evident in their nature, as the eye of an owl is related to the sun."[4]

---

[4] Aristotle, *Metaphysics, Ia,* 1 (993b 9).

(7) Sacred Scripture also gives testimony to this truth. We read in Job: "Peradventure thou wilt comprehend the steps of God, and wilt find out the Almighty perfectly?" (11:7). And again: "Behold, God is great, exceeding our knowledge" (Job 36:26). And St. Paul: "We know in part" (I Cor. 13:9).

(8) We should not, therefore, immediately reject as false, following the opinion of the Manicheans and many unbelievers, everything that is said about God even though it cannot be investigated by reason.

CHAPTER IV.   THAT THE TRUTH ABOUT GOD TO WHICH THE NATURAL REASON REACHES IS FITTINGLY PROPOSED TO MEN FOR BELIEF

(1) Since, therefore, there exists a twofold truth concerning the divine being, one to which the inquiry of the reason can reach, the other which surpasses the whole ability of the human reason, it is fitting that both of these truths be proposed to man divinely for belief. This point must first be shown concerning the truth that is open to the inquiry of the reason; otherwise, it might perhaps seem to someone that, since such a truth can be known by the reason, it was uselessly given to men through a supernatural inspiration as an object of belief.

(2) Yet, if this truth were left solely as a matter of inquiry for the human reason, three awkward consequences would follow.

(3) The first is that few men would possess the knowledge of God. For there are three reasons why most men are cut off from the fruit of diligent inquiry which is the discovery of truth. Some do not have the physical disposition for such work. As a result, there are many who are naturally not fitted to pursue knowledge; and so, however much they tried, they would be unable to reach the highest level of human knowledge which consists in knowing God. Others are cut off from pursuing this truth by the necessities imposed upon them by their daily lives. For some men must devote themselves to taking care of temporal matters. Such men would not be able to give so much time to the leisure of contemplative inquiry as to reach the highest peak at which human investigation can arrive, namely, the knowledge of God. Finally, there are some who are cut off by indolence. In order to know the things that the reason can investigate concerning God, a knowledge of many things must already be possessed. For almost all of philosophy is directed towards the knowledge of God, and that is why metaphysics, which deals with divine things, is the last part of philosophy to be learned. This means that we are able to arrive at the inquiry concerning the aforementioned truth only on the basis of a great deal of labor spent in study. Now, those who wish to undergo such a labor for the mere love of knowledge are few, even though God has inserted into the minds of men a natural appetite for knowledge.

(4) The second awkward effect is that those who would come to discover the abovementioned truth would barely reach it after a great deal of time. The reasons are several. There is the profundity of this truth, which the human intellect is made capable of grasping by natural inquiry only after a long training. Then, there are many things that must be presupposed, as we have said. There is also the fact that, in youth, when the soul is swayed by the various movements of the passions, it is not in a suitable state for the knowledge of such lofty truth. On the contrary, "one be-

come wise and knowing in repose," as it is said in the *Physics*.[5] The result is this. If the only way open to us for the knowledge of God were solely that of the reason, the human race would remain in the blackest shadows of ignorance. For then the knowledge of God, which especially renders men perfect and good, would come to be possessed only by a few, and these few would require a great deal of time in order to reach it.

(5) The third awkward effect is this. The investigation of the human reason for the most part has falsity present within it, and this is due partly to the weakness of our intellect in judgment, and partly to the admixture of images. The result is that many, remaining ignorant of the power of demonstration, would hold in doubt those things that have been most truly demonstrated. This would be particularly the case since they see that, among those who are reputed to be wise men, each one teaches his own brand of doctrine. Furthermore, with the many truths that are demonstrated, there sometimes is mingled something that is false, which is not demonstrated but rather asserted on the basis of some probable or sophistical argument, which yet has the credit of being a demonstration. That is why it was necessary that the unshakeable certitude and pure truth concerning divine things should be presented to men by way of faith.[6]

(6) Beneficially, therefore, did the divine Mercy provide that it should instruct us to hold by faith even those truths that the human reason is able to investigate. In this way, all men would easily be able to have a share in the knowledge of God, and this without uncertainty and error.

(7) Hence it is written: "Henceforward you walk not as also the Gentiles walk in the vanity of their mind, having their understanding darkened" (Eph. 4:17–18). And again: "All thy children shall be taught of the Lord" (Isa. 54:13).

CHAPTER V.   THAT THE TRUTHS THE HUMAN REASON IS NOT ABLE TO INVESTIGATE ARE FITTINGLY PROPOSED TO MEN FOR BELIEF

(1) Now, perhaps some will think that men should not be asked to believe what the reason is not adequate to investigate, since the divine Wisdom provides in the case of each thing according to the mode of its nature. We must therefore prove that it is necessary for man to receive from God as objects of belief even those truths that are above the human reason.

(2) No one tends with desire and zeal towards something that is not already known to him. But, as we shall examine later on in this work, men are ordained by the divine Providence towards a higher good than human fragility can experience in the present life.[7] That is why it was necessary for the human mind to be called to

---

[5] Aristotle, *Physics,* VII, 3 (247b 9).

[6] Although St. Thomas does not name Maimonides or his *Guide for the Perplexed (Dux neutorum)*, there are evident points of contact between the Catholic and the Jewish theologian. On the reasons for revelation given here, on our knowledge of God, on creation and the eternity of the world, and on Aristotelianism in general, St. Thomas has Maimonides in mind both to agree and to disagree with him. By way of background for SCG, I, the reader can usefully consult the references to Maimonides in E. Gilson, *History of Christian Philosophy in the Middle Ages* (New York, 1955), pp. 649–651.

[7] *SCG,* III, ch. 48.

something higher than the human reason here and now can reach, so that it would thus learn to desire something and with zeal tend towards something that surpasses the whole state of the present life. This belongs especially to the Christian religion, which in a unique way promises spiritual and eternal goods. And so there are many things proposed to men in it that transcend human sense. The Old Law, on the other hand, whose promises were of a temporal character, contained very few proposals that transcended the inquiry of the human reason. Following this same direction, the philosophers themselves, in order that they might lead men from the pleasure of sensible things to virtue, were concerned to show that there were in existence other goods of a higher nature than these things of sense, and that those who gave themselves to the active or contemplative virtues would find much sweeter enjoyment in the taste of these higher goods.

(3) It is also necessary that such truth be proposed to men for belief so that they may have a truer knowledge of God. For then only do we know God truly when we believe Him to be above everything that it is possible for man to think about Him; for, as we have shown,[8] the divine substance surpasses the natural knowledge of which man is capable. Hence, by the fact that some things about God are proposed to man that surpass his reason, there is strengthened in man the view that God is something above what he can think.

(4) Another benefit that comes from the revelation to men of truths that exceed the reason is the curbing of presumption, which is the mother of error. For there are some who have such a presumptuous opinion of their own ability that they deem themselves able to measure the nature of everything; I mean to say that, in their estimation, everything is true that seems to them so, and everything is false that does not. So that the human mind, therefore, might be freed from this presumption and come to a humble inquiry after truth, it was necessary that some things should be proposed to man by God that would completely surpass his intellect.

(5) A still further benefit may also be seen in what Aristotle says in the *Ethics*.[9] There was a certain Simonides who exhorted people to put aside the knowledge of divine things and to apply their talents to human occupations. He said that "he who is a man should know human things, and he who is mortal, things that are mortal." Against Simonides Aristotle says that "man should draw himself towards what is immortal and divine as much as he can." And so he says in the *De animalibus* that, although what we know of the higher substances is very little, yet that little is loved and desired more than all the knowledge that we have about less noble substances.[10] He also says in the *De caelo et mundo* that when questions about the heavenly bodies can be given even a modest and merely plausible solution, he who hears this experiences intense joy.[11] From all these considerations it is clear that even the most imperfect knowledge about the most noble realities brings the greatest perfection to

---

[8] See above, ch. 3.

[9] Aristotle, *Nicomachean Ethics*, X, 7 (1177b 31).

[10] Aristotle, *De partibus animalium*, I, 5 (644b 32).

[11] Aristotle, *De caelo et mundo*, II, 12 (291b 26).

the soul. Therefore, although the human reason cannot grasp fully the truths that are above it, yet, if it somehow holds these truths at least by faith, it acquires great perfection for itself.

(6) Therefore it is written: "For many things are shown to thee above the understanding of men" (Ecclus. 3:25). Again, "So the things that are of God no man knoweth but the Spirit of God. But to us God hath revealed them by His Spirit" (I Cor. 2:11, 10).

CHAPTER VI.   THAT TO GIVE ASSENT TO THE TRUTHS OF FAITH IS NOT FOOLISHNESS EVEN THOUGH THEY ARE ABOVE REASON

(1) Those who place their faith in this truth, however, "for which the human reason offers no experimental evidence,"[12] do not believe foolishly, as though "following artificial fables" (II Peter 1:16). For these "secrets of divine Wisdom" (Job 11:6) the divine Wisdom itself, which knows all things to the full, has deigned to reveal to men. It reveals its own presence, as well as the truth of its teaching and inspiration, by fitting arguments; and in order to confirm those truths that exceed natural knowledge, it gives visible manifestation to works that surpass the ability of all nature. Thus, there are the wonderful cures of illnesses, there is the raising of the dead, and the wonderful immutation in the heavenly bodies; and what is more wonderful, there is the inspiration given to human minds, so that simple and untutored persons, filled with the gift of the Holy Spirit, come to possess instantaneously the highest wisdom and the readiest eloquence. When these arguments were examined, through the efficacy of the above-mentioned proof, and not the violent assault of arms or the promise of pleasures, and (what is most wonderful of all) in the midst of the tyranny of the persecutors, an innumerable throng of people, both simple and most learned, flocked to the Christian faith. In this faith there are truths preached that surpass every human intellect; the pleasures of the flesh are curbed; it is taught that the things of the world should be spurned. Now, for the minds of mortal men to assent to these things is the greatest of miracles, just as it is a manifest work of divine inspiration that, spurning visible things, men should seek only what is invisible. Now, that this has happened neither without preparation nor by chance, but as a result of the disposition of God, is clear from the fact that through many pronouncements of the ancient prophets God had foretold that He would do this. The books of these prophets are held in veneration among us Christians, since they give witness to our faith.

(2) The manner of this confirmation is touched on by St. Paul: "Which," that is, human salvation, "having begun to be declared by the Lord, was confirmed unto us by them that hear Him: God also bearing them witness of signs, and wonders, and divers miracles, and distributions of the Holy Ghost" (Heb. 2:3–4).

(3) This wonderful conversion of the world to the Christian faith is the clearest witness of the signs given in the past; so that it is not necessary that they should be further repeated, since they appear most clearly in their effect. For it would be truly

---

[12] St. Gregory, *Homiliae in evangelia,* II, hom. 26, i (*PL,* 76, col. 1197).

6

more wonderful than all signs if the world had been led by simple and humble men to believe such lofty truths, to accomplish such difficult actions, and to have such high hopes. Yet it is also a fact that, even in our own time, God does not cease to work miracles through His saints for the confirmation of the faith.

(4) On the other hand, those who founded sects committed to erroneous doctrines proceeded in a way that is opposite to this. The point is clear in the case of Mohammed. He seduced the people by promises of carnal pleasure to which the concupiscence of the flesh goads us. His teaching also contained precepts that were in conformity with his promises, and he gave free rein to carnal pleasure. In all this, as is not unexpected, he was obeyed by carnal men. As for proofs of the truth of his doctrine, he brought forward only such as could be grasped by the natural ability of anyone with a very modest wisdom. Indeed, the truths that he taught he mingled with many fables and with doctrines of the greatest falsity. He did not bring forth any signs produced in a supernatural way, which alone fittingly gives witness to divine inspiration; for a visible action that can be only divine reveals an invisibly inspired teacher of truth. On the contrary, Mohammed said that he was sent in the power of his arms—which are signs not lacking even to robbers and tyrants. What is more, no wise men, men trained in things divine and human, believed in him from the beginning. Those who believed in him were brutal men and desert wanderers, utterly ignorant of all divine teaching, through whose numbers Mohammed forced others to become his followers by the violence of his arms. Nor do divine pronouncements on the part of preceding prophets offer him any witness. On the contrary, he perverts almost all the testimonies of the Old and New Testaments by making them into fabrications of his own, as can be seen by anyone who examines his law. It was, therefore, a shrewd decision on his part to forbid his followers to read the Old and New Testaments, lest these books convict him of falsity. It is thus clear that those who place any faith in his words believe foolishly.

CHAPTER VII.   THAT THE TRUTH OF REASON IS NOT OPPOSED TO THE TRUTH OF THE CHRISTIAN FAITH

(1) Now, although the truth of the Christian faith which we have discussed surpasses the capacity of the reason, nevertheless that truth that the human reason is naturally endowed to know cannot be opposed to the truth of the Christian faith. For that with which the human reason is naturally endowed is clearly most true; so much so, that it is impossible for us to think of such truths as false. Nor is it permissible to believe as false that which we hold by faith, since this is confirmed in a way that is so clearly divine. Since, therefore, only the false is opposed to the true, as is clearly evident from an examination of their definitions, it is impossible that the truth of faith should be opposed to those principles that the human reason knows naturally.

(2) Furthermore, that which is introduced into the soul of the student by the teacher is contained in the knowledge of the teacher—unless his teaching is fictitious, which it is improper to say of God. Now, the knowledge of the principles that are known to us naturally has been implanted in us by God; for God is the Author of our nature. These principles, therefore, are also contained by the divine Wisdom.

Hence, whatever is opposed to them is opposed to the divine Wisdom, and, therefore, cannot come from God. That which we hold by faith as divinely revealed, therefore, cannot be contrary to our natural knowledge.

(3) Again. In the presence of contrary arguments our intellect is chained, so that it cannot proceed to the knowledge of the truth. If, therefore, contrary knowledges were implanted in us by God, our intellect would be hindered from knowing truth by this very fact. Now, such an effect cannot come from God.

(4) And again. What is natural cannot change as long as nature does not. Now, it is impossible that contrary opinions should exist in the same knowing subject at the same time. No opinion or belief, therefore, is implanted in man by God which is contrary to man's natural knowledge.

(5) Therefore, the Apostle says: "The word is nigh thee, even in thy mouth and in thy heart. This is the word of faith, which we preach" (Rom. 10:8). But because it overcomes reason, there are some who think that it is opposed to it: which is impossible.

(6) The authority of St. Augustine also agrees with this. He writes as follows: "That which truth will reveal cannot in any way be opposed to the sacred books of the Old and the New Testament." [13]

(7) From this we evidently gather the following conclusion: whatever arguments are brought forward against the doctrines of faith are conclusions incorrectly derived from the first and self-evident principles imbedded in nature. Such conclusions do not have the force of demonstration; they are arguments that are either probable or sophistical. And so, there exists the possibility to answer them.

CHAPTER VIII.   HOW THE HUMAN REASON IS RELATED TO THE TRUTH OF FAITH

(1) There is also a further consideration. Sensible things, from which the human reason takes the origin of its knowledge, retain within themselves some sort of trace of a likeness to God. This is so imperfect, however, that it is absolutely inadequate to manifest the substance of God. For effects bear within themselves, in their own way, the likeness of their causes, since an agent produces its like; yet an effect does not always reach to the full likeness of its cause. Now, the human reason is related to the knowledge of the truth of faith (a truth which can be most evident only to those who see the divine substance) in such a way that it can gather certain likenesses of it, which are yet not sufficient so that the truth of faith may be comprehended as being understood demonstratively or through itself. Yet it is useful for the human reason to exercise itself in such arguments, however weak they may be, provided only that there be present no presumption to comprehend or to demonstrate. For to be able to see something of the loftiest realities, however thin and weak the sight may be, is, as our previous remarks indicate, a cause of the greatest joy.

(2) The testimony of Hilary agrees with this. Speaking of this same truth, he writes as follows in his *De Trinitate:* "Enter these truths by believing, press forward,

---

[13] St. Augustine, *De genesi ad litteram,* II, c. 18 (*PL,* 34, col. 280).

persevere. And though I may know that you will not arrive at an end, yet I will congratulate you in your progress. For, though he who pursues the infinite with reverence will never finally reach the end, yet he will always progress by pressing onward. But do not intrude yourself into the divine secret, do not, presuming to comprehend the sum total of intelligence, plunge yourself into the mystery of the unending nativity; rather, understand that these things are incomprehensible."[14]

---

[14] St. Hilary, *De Trinitate*, II, 10, ii (*PL*, 10, coll. 58–59).

CHAPTER VIII

How He is both merciful and impassible

BUT how are You at once both merciful and impassible? For
if You are impassible You do not have any compassion; and if
You have no compassion Your heart is not sorrowful from
compassion with the sorrowful, which is what being merciful is.
But if You are not merciful whence comes so much consolation
for the sorrowful?

How, then, are You merciful and not merciful, O Lord,
unless it be that You are merciful in relation to us and not in
relation to Yourself? In fact, You are [merciful] according to our
way of looking at things and not according to Your way. For
when You look upon us in our misery it is we who feel the
effect of Your mercy, but You do not experience the feeling.
Therefore You are both merciful because You save the sorrowful and pardon sinners against You; and You are not merciful
because You do not experience any feeling of compassion for
misery.

QUESTION 9

The Immutability of God

(In Two Articles)

WE next consider God's immutability, and His eternity following on His immutability.

On the immutability of God there are two points of inquiry: (1) Whether God is altogether immutable? (2) Whether to be immutable belongs to God alone?

FIRST ARTICLE

Whether God Is Altogether Immutable?

We proceed thus to the First Article:—

Objection 1. It seems that God is not altogether immutable. For whatever moves itself is in some way mutable. But, as Augustine says (*Gen. ad lit,* viii. 20), *The Creator Spirit moves Himself neither by time, nor by place.* Therefore God is in some way mutable.

Obj. 2. Further, it is said of Wisdom, that *it is more mobile than all things active*—Vulg. *mobilior.* (Wisd. vii. 24). But God is wisdom itself; therefore God is movable.

Obj. 3. Further, to approach and to recede signify movement. But these are said of God in Scripture, *Draw nigh to God, and He will draw nigh to you* (James iv. 8). Therefore God is mutable.

On the contrary, It is written, *I am the Lord, and I change not* (Mal. iii. 6).

I answer that, From what precedes, it is shown that God is altogether immutable. First, because it was shown above that there is some first being, whom we call God; and that this first being must be pure act, without the admixture of any potentiality, for the reason that, absolutely, potentiality is posterior to act. Now everything which is in any way changed, is in some way in potentiality. Hence it is evident that it is impossible for God to be in any way changeable. Secondly, because everything which is moved, remains as it was in part, and passes away in part; as what is moved from whiteness to blackness, remains the same as to substance; thus in everything which is moved, there is some kind of composition to be found. But it has been shown above (Q. 3, A. 7) that in God there is no composition, for He is altogether simple. Hence it is manifest that God cannot be moved. Thirdly, because everything which is moved acquires something by its movement, and attains to what it had not attained previously. But since God is infinite, comprehending in Himself all the plenitude of perfection of all being, He cannot acquire anything new, nor extend Himself to anything whereto He was not extended previously. Hence movement in no way belongs to Him. So, some of the ancients, constrained, as it were, by the truth, decided that the first principle was immovable.

Reply Obj. 1. Augustine there speaks in a similar way to Plato, who said that the first mover moves Himself; calling every operation a movement, even as the acts of understanding, and willing, and loving, are called movements. Therefore because God understands and loves Himself, in that respect they said that God moves Himself, not, however, as movement and change belong to a thing existing in potentiality, as we now speak of change and movement.

Reply Obj. 2. Wisdom is called mobile by way of similitude, according as it diffuses its likeness even to the outermost of things; for nothing can exist which does not proceed from the divine wisdom by way of some kind of imitation, as from the first effective and formal principle; as also works of art proceed from the wisdom of the artist. And so in the same way, inasmuch as the similitude of the divine wisdom proceeds in degrees from the highest things, which participate more fully of its likeness, to the lowest things which participate of it in a lesser degree, there is said be a kind of procession and movement of the divine wisdom to things; as when we say that the sun proceeds to the earth, inasmuch as the ray of light touches the earth. In this way Dionysius (*Cœl. Hier.* i) expounds the matter, that every procession of the divine manifestation comes to us from the movement of the Father of light.

Reply Obj. 3. These things are said of God in Scripture metaphorically. For as the sun is said to enter a house, or to go out, according as its rays reach the house, so God is said to approach to us, or to recede from us, when we receive the influx of His goodness, or decline from Him.

SECOND ARTICLE

Whether to Be Immutable Belongs to God Alone?

We proceed thus to the Second Article:—

Objection 1. It seems that to be immutable does not belong to God alone. For the Philosopher says (*Metaph.* ii), that *matter is in everything which is moved.* But, according to some, certain created substances, as angels and souls, have not matter. Therefore to be immutable does not belong to God alone.

Obj. 2. Further, everything in motion moves to some end. What therefore has already attained its ultimate end, is not in motion. But some creatures have already attained to their ultimate end; as all the blessed in heaven. Therefore some creatures are immovable.

Obj. 3. Further, everything which is mutable, is variable. But forms are invariable; for it is said (*Sex Princip.* i) that *form is essence consisting of the simple and invariable.* Therefore it does not belong to God alone to be immutable.

On the contrary, Augustine says (*De Nat. Boni.* i.), *God alone is immutable; and whatever things He has made, being from nothing, are mutable.*

I answer that, God alone is altogether immutable; whereas, every creature is in some way mutable. Be it known therefore that a mutable thing can be called so in two ways; by a power in itself; and by a power possessed by another. For all creatures before they existed, were possible, not by any created power, since no creature is eternal, but by the divine power alone, inasmuch as God could produce them into existence. Thus, as the production of a thing into existence depends on the will of God, so likewise it depends on His will that things should be preserved; for He does not preserve them otherwise than by ever giving them existence; hence if He took away His action from them, all things would be reduced to nothing, as appears from Augustine (*Gen. ad lit.* iv. 12). Therefore as it was in the Creator's power to produce them before they existed in themselves; so likewise it is in the Creator's power when they exist in themselves to bring them to nothing. In this way therefore, by the power of another—namely, of God—they are mutable, inasmuch as they are producible from nothing by Him, and are by Him reducible from existence to non-existence.

If, however, a thing is called mutable by a power in itself, thus also in some manner every creature is mutable. For every creature has a twofold power, active and passive; and I call that power passive which enables anything to attain its perfection either in being, or in attaining to its end. Now if the mutability of a thing be considered according to its power for being, in that way all creatures are not mutable, but those only in which what is potential in them is consistent with non-being. Hence, in the inferior bodies there is mutability both as regards substantial being, inasmuch as their matter can exist with privation of their substantial form, and also as regards their accidental being, supposing the subject to coexist with privation of accident; as, for example, this subject *man* can exist with *not-whiteness,* and can therefore be changed from white to not-white. But supposing the accident to be such as to follow on the essential principles of the subject, then the privation of such an accident cannot coexist with the subject. Hence the subject cannot be changed as regards that kind of accident; as, for example, snow cannot be made black. Now in the celestial bodies matter is not consistent with privation of form, because the form perfects the whole potentiality of the matter; therefore these bodies are not mutable as to substantial being, but only as to locality, because the subject is consistent with privation of this or that place. On the other hand incorporeal substances, being subsistent forms which, although with respect to their own existence are as potentiality to act, are not consistent with the privation of this act; forasmuch as existence is consequent upon form, and nothing corrupts except it lose its form. Hence in the form itself there is no power to non-existence; and so these kinds of substances are immutable and invariable as regards their existence. Wherefore Dionysius says (*Div. Nom.* iv), that *intellectual created substances are pure from generation and from every variation, as also are incorporeal and immaterial substances.* Still, there remains in them a twofold mutability: one as regards their potentiality to their end; and in that way there is in them a mutability according to choice from good to evil, as Damascene says (*De Fide,* ii. 3, 4); the other as regards place, inasmuch as by their finite power they attain to certain fresh places—which cannot be said of God, who by His infinity fills all places, as was shown above (Q. 8. A. 2).

Thus in every creature there is a potentiality to change either as regards substantial being as in the case of things corruptible; or as regards locality only, as in the case of the celestial bodies; or as regards the order to their end, and the application of their powers to divers objects, as is the case with the angels; and universally all creatures generally are mutable by the power of the Creator, in Whose power is their existence and non-existence. Hence since God is in none of these ways mutable, it belongs to Him alone to be altogether immutable.

Reply Obj. 1. This objection proceeds from mutability as regards substantial or accidental being; for philosophers treated of such movement.

Reply Obj. 2. The good angels, besides their natural endowment of immutability of being, have also immutability of election by divine power; nevertheless there remains in them mutability as regards place.

Reply Obj. 3. Forms are called invariable, forasmuch as they cannot be subjects of variation; but they are subject to variation because by them their subject is variable. Hence it is clear that they vary in so far as they are; for they are not called beings as though they were the subject of being, but because through them something has being.

4. THE CONSEQUENCES IF THE ARGUMENTS FAIL

The arguments are the only way to establish theism, and they must be judged by the usual standards of evidence—this we have argued. It will now be shown that if they fail, there is no alternative to atheism.

Against this it has commonly been held that the absence of arguments *for* the existence of something is not the same as the presence of arguments *against* its existence; so agnosticism or an option remains when the arguments fail. But insofar as this is true, it is irrelevant. It is true only if we restrict "arguments for the existence of something" to highly specific demonstrations which attempt to establish their conclusion as beyond all reasonable doubt. The absence of these is indeed compatible with the conclusion's being quite likely, which would make denial of its existence unjustified. But if we take arguments for the existence of something to include all the evidence which supports the existence claim to any significant degree, i.e., makes it at all probable, then the absence of such evidence means there is *no* likelihood of the existence of the entity. And this, of course, is a complete justification for the claim that the entity does not exist, provided that the entity is not one which might leave no traces (a God who is impotent or who does not care for us), and provided that we have comprehensively examined the area where

such evidence would appear if there were any.[7] Now justifying the claim
that something does not exist is not quite the same as proving or having
arguments that it doesn't, but it is what we are talking about. That is, we
need not have a proof that God does not exist in order to justify atheism.
Atheism is obligatory in the absence of any evidence for God's existence.

Why do adults not believe in Santa Claus? Simply because they can
now explain the phenomena for which Santa Claus's existence is invoked
without any need for introducing a novel entity. When we were very young
and naïvely believed our parents' stories, it was hard to see how the presents
could get there on Christmas morning since the doors were locked and our
parents were asleep in bed. Someone *must* have brought them down the
chimney. And how could that person get to the roof without a ladder and
with all those presents? Surely only by flying. And then there is that great
traditional literature of stories and songs which immortalize the entity and
his (horned) attendants; surely these cannot all be just products of imagination? Where there is smoke, there must be fire.

Santa Claus is not a bad hypothesis at all for six-year-olds. As we grow
up, no one comes forward to *prove* that such an entity does not exist. We
just come to see that there is not the least reason to think he *does* exist. And
so it would be entirely foolish to assert that he does, or believe that he does,
or even think it likely that he does. Santa Claus is in just the same position
as fairy godmothers, wicked witches, the devil, and the ether. Each of these
entities has some supernatural powers, i.e., powers which contravene or go
far beyond the powers that we know exist, whether it be the power to levitate
a sled and reindeer or the power to cast a spell. Now even belief in something
for which there is *no* evidence, i.e., a belief which goes *beyond* the evidence,
although a lesser sin than belief in something which is *contrary* to well-
established laws, is plainly irrational in that it simply amounts to attaching
belief where it is not justified. So the proper alternative, when there is no
evidence, is not mere suspension of belief, e.g., about Santa Claus; it is
disbelief. It most certainly is not faith.

The situation is slightly different with the Abominable Snowman, sea
serpents, or even the Loch Ness monster. No "supernatural" (by which, in
this context, we only mean wholly unprecedented) kinds of powers are involved. Previous discoveries have been made of creatures which had long
seemed extinct, and from these we can immediately derive some likelihood

[7] This last proviso is really superfluous since it is built into the phrase "the absence of
such evidence," which is not the same as "ignorance of such evidence"; but it is included for the sake of clarity. When we are investigating the existence of God, we
naturally attempt to discuss all the evidence, conclusive or not; so if this comes to
naught, we would be left with no alternative to atheism. Fence sitting with the agnostic
is not only uncomfortable; it is even indefensible.

of further discoveries.[8] Footprints or disturbances for which no fully satis-
factory alternative explanation has yet been discovered (although such an
explanation is by no means impossible) have been seen in the Himalayan
snow and the Scottish lochs. It would be credulous for the layman to believe
firmly in the existence of these entities. Yet it would be equally inappropriate
to say it is certain they do not exist. Here is a domain for agnosticism (though
perhaps an agnosticism inclined toward skepticism). For the agnostic does not
believe that a commitment either way is justified, and he is surely right about
strange creatures which, while of a new *appearance,* have powers that are
mere extensions, proportional to size, of those with which we are already
familiar on this Earth. There is some suggestive, if by no means conclusive,
evidence for such entities; and the balance of general considerations is not
heavily against them.

But when the assertion is made that something exists with powers that
strikingly transcend the well-established generalizations we have formulated
about animal capacities or reasonable extrapolations from them, then we
naturally expect correspondingly better evidence before we concede that there
is a serious likelihood of having to abandon those generalizations. It is entirely appropriate to demand much stronger support for claims of telepathy or
levitation or miraculous cures than for new sports records or feats of memory
in which previous levels of performance are merely bettered to some degree,
in a way that is almost predictable. On the other hand, it is entirely prejudiced
to reject all such evidence on the ground that it *must* be deceptive because it
contravenes previously established generalizations. This is simply to deify
the present state of science; it is the precise opposite of the experimental
attitude. It is right to demand a stronger case to overthrow a strong case and
to demand very strong evidence to demonstrate unprecedented powers. It is
irrational to require that the evidence of these powers be just as commonplace
and compelling as for the previously known powers of man or beast: one
cannot legislate the exceptional into the commonplace.

We can now use a set of distinctions that would previously have seemed
very abstract. First, let us distinguish a belief which is wholly without general
or particular evidential support from one which can be directly disproved.
The claim that a race of men lives on the moons of Jupiter or that a certain
cola causes cancer of the colon is entirely unfounded but not totally impossible. The view that the ratio of a circle's circumference to its diameter can

[8] We would not normally say this general consideration is *"evidence* for the existence
of the Loch Ness monster"; evidence, like proof, must be rather specifically tied to a
claim. But these general background considerations set the stage for proofs, and they
directly determine the legitimacy of total skepticism or complete confidence. We regard them as relevant considerations, and the present claim is that without even these
no option but atheism is possible.

be expressed as a fraction is demonstrably untenable, as is the view that some living men are infinitely strong, or that any man is or has been unbeatable at chess, or that the FBI has wiped out the Mafia. We normally say that a claim is *well founded* if there is evidence which is best explained by this claim. We may say it is *provable* if the evidence is indubitable and the claim is very clearly required. If there is no evidence which points to this particular claim, although some general background considerations make it not too unlikely that something like this should be true (Loch Ness monster, mile record broken twice in 1980), we would say there is *some general support* for the claim. We shall say it is *wholly unfounded* (or *wholly unsupported*) if there is no evidence for it in particular and no general considerations in its favor, and *disprovable* if it implies that something would be the case that definitely is not the case.

Of course it is foolish to believe a claim that is disproved, but it is also foolish to believe a wholly unsupported claim, and it is still foolish even to treat such a claim as if it were worth serious consideration. A claim for which there is some general or some particular support cannot be dismissed, but neither can it be treated as established. The connection between evidential support and the appropriate degree of belief can be demonstrated as shown in the diagram on the next page, which is quite unlike the oversimplified idea that the arrangement should be:

Provable	Theism
Disprovable	Atheism
Neither	Agnosticism

The crucial difference is that both "unfounded" and "disprovable" correlate with atheism, just as the two corresponding types of provability correlate with theism; hence the agnostic's territory is smaller than he often supposes.

Recalling that to get even a little evidential support for the existence of a Being with supernatural powers will require that the little be of very high quality (*little* does not mean "dubious"), we see that the failure of all the arguments, i.e., of all the evidence, will make even agnosticism in the wide sense an indefensible exaggeration of the evidential support.[9] And agnosticism in the narrow sense will be an exaggeration unless the arguments are strong enough to establish about a 50 per cent probability for the claim of theism. Apart from the wide and narrow senses of agnosticism there is also a distinction between a positive agnostic and a negative agnostic.

[9] Technical note: Attempts to formulate the general principle of evidence involved have usually run into difficulties related to those made familiar in the discussions of the paradoxes of confirmation. For example, negative existential hypotheses in natural language can be supported by the failure of proofs of their contradictories, but positive existential hypotheses are not made plausible by the failure of disproofs of their denials.

EVIDENTIAL SITUATION	APPROPRIATE ATTITUDE	NAME FOR APPROPRIATE ATTITUDE IN THEISM CASE	
1. Strictly disprovable, i.e., demonstrably incompatible with the evidence.	Rejection	Atheism	
2. Wholly unfounded, i.e., wholly lacking in general or particular support.			
3. Possessing some general or particular support; still improbable.	Skepticism but recognition as a real *possibility*; not to be wholly disregarded in comprehensive planning but to be bet *against*.	Skepticism	Agnosticism (wide sense)
4. Possessing substantial support but with substantial alternatives still open; a balance of evidence for and against; about 50 per cent probable.	Suspension of judgment. Make no commitment either way; treat each alternative as approximately equally serious.	Agnosticism (narrow sense)	
5. Possessing powerful evidential support; some difficulties of inadequacies or significant alternatives remaining; probable.	Treat as probably true; bet *on*.	Pragmatic theism	
6. Possessing overwhelming particular support and no basis for alternative views; beyond reasonable doubt; provable in the usual sense.	Acceptance	Theism	
7. Strictly provable, i.e., as a demonstrably necessary result of indubitable facts.			

21

A *positive agnostic* maintains that the evidence is such as to make his position the correct one and those of the theist and atheist incorrect. *Negative agnosticism* is simply the position of not accepting either theism or atheism; it does not suggest that they are both wrong—it may be just an expression of felt indecision or ignorance. The difference between negative and positive agnosticism is like the difference between a *neutral* who says, "I don't know who's right—maybe one of the disputants, or maybe neither," and a *third force* who says, "Neither is right, and I have a third alternative which *is* right." Obviously, the negative agnostic has not progressed as far in his thinking as the positive agnostic, in one sense, because he has not been able to decide which of the three possible positions is correct. The view of the negative agnostic cannot be right, but his position may be the right position for some-one who has not thought the matter through or who lacks the capacity to do so.

In practice, an agnostic's position is often the product of an untidy mixture of factors. He may never have happened to come across an argument for either theism or atheism which struck him as compelling; a rough head counting has revealed intelligent people on either side; his nose for social stigmas indicates a slight odor of intellectual deficiency attached to theism by contemporary intellectuals and a suggestion of unnecessary boat rocking or perhaps rabid subversion attached to atheism. This makes the agnostic fence look pretty attractive; so up he climbs, to sit on top. But now we put the challenge to him. Is he incapable of thinking out an answer for himself? If so, he is intellectually inferior to those below; if not, he must descend and demonstrate the failings of the contestants before he is entitled to his perch. Agnosticism as a position is interesting and debatable; agnosticism as the absence of a position is simply a sign of the absence of intellectual activity or capacity.

1

The tao that can be told
is not the eternal Tao.
The name that can be named
is not the eternal Name.

The unnamable is the eternally real.
Naming is the origin
of all particular things.

Free from desire, you realize the mystery.
Caught in desire, you see only the manifestations.

Yet mystery and manifestations
arise from the same source.
This source is called darkness.

Darkness within darkness.
The gateway to all understanding.

2

When people see some things as beautiful,
other things become ugly.
When people see some things as good,
other things become bad.

Being and non-being create each other.
Difficult and easy support each other.
Long and short define each other.
High and low depend on each other.
Before and after follow each other.

Therefore the Master
acts without doing anything
and teaches without saying anything.
Things arise and she lets them come;
things disappear and she lets them go.
She has but doesn't possess,
acts but doesn't expect.
When her work is done, she forgets it.
That is why it lasts forever.

14

Look, and it can't be seen.
Listen, and it can't be heard.
Reach, and it can't be grasped.

Above, it isn't bright.
Below, it isn't dark.
Seamless, unnamable,
it returns to the realm of nothing.
Form that includes all forms,
image without an image,
subtle, beyond all conception.

Approach it and there is no beginning;
follow it and there is no end.
You can't know it, but you can be it,
at ease in your own life.
Just realize where you come from:
this is the essence of wisdom.

25

There was something formless and perfect
before the universe was born.
It is serene. Empty.
Solitary. Unchanging.
Infinite. Eternally present.
It is the mother of the universe.
For lack of a better name,
I call it the Tao.

It flows through all things,
inside and outside, and returns
to the origin of all things.

The Tao is great.
The universe is great.
Earth is great.
Man is great.
These are the four great powers.

Man follows the earth.
Earth follows the universe.
The universe follows the Tao.
The Tao follows only itself.

Chapter 1
Six Common Mistakes about God

The Mistakes Briefly Presented

IN THIS SECTION I introduce, with a minimum of criticism or argument, six ideas about God which have been held by a great number of learned and brilliant philosophers and theologians through many centuries and in many religious traditions, but which I and many others, including some distinguished modern theologians and philosophers, have found quite unacceptable. In other words, what we attack is an old tradition, but we attack it standing within a somewhat newer tradition. In this newer tradition there is a partial appeal (with reservations) to still a third tradition which is old indeed, expressed in various sacred writings, including the Old and New Testaments of the Bible. For it is our contention that the "theological mistakes" in question give the word *God* a meaning which is not true to its import in sacred writings or in concrete religious piety. This result came about partly because theologians in medieval Europe and the Near East were somewhat learned in Greek philosophy and largely ignorant of any other philosophy. This happened in both Christianity and Islam, to a somewhat lesser extent in Judaism. In all three religions there was a development of mysticism, which was different still and in some ways partially corrective of the all-too-Greek form taken by the official theologies.

In section B, I develop at length my arguments against the six mistakes, which together form what I call classical theism (the one too strongly influenced by Greek philosophy as medieval scholars knew that philosophy) and in favor of what I sometimes call the

1

new theism, sometimes process theology, sometimes neoclassical theism—which is my version of a general point of view that has had a good many proponents in recent times.

First Mistake: God Is Absolutely Perfect and Therefore Unchangeable. In Plato's *Republic* one finds the proposition: God, being perfect, cannot change (not for the better, since "perfect" means that there can be no better; not for the worse, since ability to change for the worse, to decay, degenerate, or become corrupt, is a weakness, an imperfection). The argument may seem cogent, but it is so only if two assumptions are valid: that it is possible to conceive of a meaning for "perfect" that excludes change in any and every respect and that we must conceive God as perfect in just *this* sense. Obviously the ordinary meanings of perfect do not entirely exclude change. Thus Wordsworth wrote of his wife that she was a "perfect woman," but he certainly did not mean that she was totally unchangeable. In many places in the Bible human beings are spoken of as perfect; again the entire exclusion of change cannot have been intended. Where in the Bible God is spoken of as perfect, the indications are that even here the exclusion of change in any and every respect was not implied. And where God is directly spoken of as strictly unchanging ("without shadow of turning"), there is still a possibility of ambiguity. God might be absolutely unchangeable in righteousness (which is what the context indicates is the intended meaning), but changeable in ways compatible with, neutral to, *or even required by*, this unswerving constancy in righteousness. Thus, God would be in no degree, however slight, alterable in the respect in question (the divine steadfastness in good will) and yet alterable, not necessarily in spite of, but even because of, this steadfastness. If the creatures behave according to God's will, God will appreciate this behavior; if not, God will have a different response, equally appropriate and expressive of the divine goodness.

The Biblical writers were not discussing Greek philosophical issues, and it is at our own peril that we interpret them as if they were discussing these, just as it is at our peril if we take them to be discussing various modern issues that had not arisen in ancient Palestine. It may even turn out on inquiry that perfection, if taken to imply an absolute maximum of value in *every conceivable respect,*

does not make sense or is contradictory. In that case the argument of the *Republic* is an argument from an absurdity and proves nothing. Logicians have found that abstract definitions may seem harmless and yet be contradictory when their meanings are spelled out. Example, "the class of all classes." Similarly, "actuality of all possible values," to which no addition is possible, may have contradictory implications. If perfection cannot consistently mean this value maximum, then the Platonic argument is unsound. Nor was it necessarily Plato's last word on the subject. (See Chapter 2B.)

Second Mistake: Omnipotence. God, being defined as perfect in all respects must, it seems, be perfect in power; therefore, whatever happens is divinely made to happen. If I die of cancer this misfortune is God's doing. The question then becomes,, "Why has God done this to me?" Here everything depends on "perfect in power" or "omnipotent." And here, too, there are possible ambiguities, as we shall see.

Third Mistake: Omniscience. Since God is unchangeably perfect, whatever happens must be eternally known to God. Our tomorrow's deeds, not yet decided upon by us, are yet always or eternally present to God, for whom there is no open future. Otherwise (the argument goes), God would be "ignorant," imperfect in knowledge, waiting to observe what we may do. Hence, whatever freedom of decision we may have must be somehow reconciled with the alleged truth that our decisions bring about no additions to the divine life. Here perfect and unchanging knowledge, free from ignorance or increase, are the key terms. It can be shown that they are all seriously lacking in clarity, and that the theological tradition resolved the ambiguities in a question-begging way.

It is interesting that the idea of an unchangeable omniscience covering every detail of the world's history is not to be found definitely stated in ancient Greek philosophy (unless in Stoicism, which denied human freedom) and is rejected by Aristotle. It is not clearly affirmed in the Bible. It is inconspicuous in the philosophies of India, China, and Japan. Like the idea of omnipotence, it is largely an invention of Western thought of the Dark or Middle Ages. It still goes unchallenged in much current religious thought.

But many courageous and competent thinkers have rejected it, including Schelling and Whitehead.

Fourth Mistake: God's Unsympathetic Goodness. God's "love" for us does not, for classical theists, mean that God sympathizes with us, is rejoiced or made happy by our joy or good fortune or grieved by our sorrow or misery. Rather God's love is like the sun's way of doing good, which benefits the myriad forms of life on earth but receives no benefits from the good it produces. Nor does the sun lose anything by its activity (we now know that this is bad astronomy). Or, God's beneficial activity is like that of an over-flowing fountain that remains forever full no matter how much water comes from it, and without receiving any from outside. Thus it is not human love, even at its best, that was taken as the model for divine love but instead two inanimate phenomena of nature, fictitiously conceived at that. Bad physics and astronomy, rather than sound psychology, were the sources of the imagery.

In short, argument from an insufficiently analyzed notion of perfection and a preference for materialistic (and prescientific) rather than truly spiritual conceptions were for almost two thousand years dominant in Western theology.

Fifth Mistake: Immortality as a Career after Death. If our existence has any importance for God, or if God loves us, He-She will not—it was argued—allow death to turn us into mere corpses. Hence, many have concluded, a theist must believe that we survive death in some form, and that the myths of heaven and hell have some truth in them. Here the assumption is that a mere corpse on the one hand and on the other hand survival in a new mode of heavenly or hellish existence (in which our individual consciousnesses will have *new* experiences not enjoyed or suffered while on earth) are the only possibilities. There is, however, as we shall see, a third possibility, quite compatible with God's love for us.

It is notable that in most of the Old Testament, for instance in the sublime Book of Job, individual immortality is not even men-tioned. To this day, religious Judaism is much more cautious about affirming, and it often denies, such immortality. In the New Tes-tament Jesus says little that seems to bear on the subject, and

according to at least one very distinguished theologian (Reinhold Niebuhr), even that little is not decisive in excluding the third possibility just mentioned.

Sixth Mistake: Revelation as Infallible. The idea of revelation is the idea of special knowledge of God, or of religious truth, possessed by some people and transmitted by them to others. In some form or other the idea is reasonable. In all other matters people differ in their degree of skill or insight. Why not in religion? In the various sciences we acknowledge some people as experts and regard their opinions as of more value than those of the rest of us. The notion that in religion there are no individuals whose insight is any clearer, deeper, or more authentic than anyone else's is not particularly plausible. In all countries and in all historical times there have been individuals to whom multitudes have looked for guidance in religion. Buddha, Lao Tse, Confucius, Moses, Zoroaster, Shankara, Jesus, Muhammed, Joseph Smith, and Mary Baker Eddy were such individuals. New examples are to be found within the lives of many of us. Pure democracy or sheer equalitarianism in religious matters is not to be expected of our human nature. Some distinction between leaders or founders and followers or disciples seems to be our destiny. But there is a question of degree, or of qualification. To what extent, or under what conditions, are some individuals, or perhaps is some unique individual, worthy of trust in religious matters? It is in the answer to this question that mistakes can be made. Only a few years ago such a mistake sent hundreds to death, partly at their own hands, at Jonestown in British Guiana.

In religions that think of God as a conscious, purposive being, the idea of revelation can take a special form. Not simply that some are abler, wiser, than others in religion, as individuals may be in a science or in politics, but that divine wisdom has selected and so controlled a certain individual or set of individuals as to make them transmitters of the very wisdom of God to humanity. Since God is infallible (can make no mistakes), if no limitations are admitted to this conception of revelation, the distinction between fallible human beings and the infallible God tends to disappear. And so we find letters to newspaper editors in which the writer claims that his or her quotation from the Bible supporting some political position has the backing of "God almighty." Thus the essential principle of democracy, that none of us is divinely wise, that we all may make mistakes, is compromised.

One defence of claims to revelation is the reported occurrence of miracles. The fact, however, is that in every religion miracles are claimed. Hence the mere claim is not enough to establish the validity of the revelation. Buddha is reported to have spoken as a newborn infant. Was Shotoku Taishi, ruler-saint of seventh century Japan, shown to be of superordinary status by the fact that his death brought forth "rain from a cloudless sky"? Unless one believes (or disbelieves) all such accounts, how does one know where to stop?

What Went Wrong in Classical Theism

Two Meanings of "God Is Perfect and Unchanging." The word 'perfect' literally means "completely made" or "finished." But God is conceived as the maker or creator of all; so what could have made God (whether or not the making was properly completed)? 'Perfect' seems a poor word to describe the divine reality.

To describe something as "not perfect" seems a criticism, it implies fault finding; worship excludes criticism and fault finding. God is to be "loved with all one's mind, heart, and soul." Such love seems to rule out the possibility of criticism. Suppose we accept this. Do we then have to admit that God cannot change? Clearly yes, insofar as change is for the worse and capacity for it objectionable, a *fault or weakness*. God then cannot change for the worse. The view I wish to defend admits this. But does every conceivable kind of change show a fault or weakness? Is there not change for the better? We praise people when they change in this fashion. All healthy growth is such change. We are delighted in growth in infants and children. Is there nothing to learn from this about how to conceive God?

It is easy to reply that, whereas the human offspring starts as a mere fertilized single cell and before that as an unfertilized one, God is surely not to be so conceived. However, no analogy between something human and the worshipful God is to be taken in simple-

minded literalness. There still may be an analogy between growth as a wholly good form of change and the divine life. For it is arguable that even an infinite richness may be open to increase. The great logician Bertrand Russell expressed this opinion to me, although Russell was an atheist and had no interest in supporting my, or any, theology.

The traditional objection, already mentioned, to divine change was that if a being were already perfect, meaning that nothing better were possible, then change for the better must be impossible for the being. The unnoticed assumption here has been (for two thousand and more years) that it makes sense to think of a value so great or marvelous that it could in no sense whatever be excelled or surpassed. How do we know that this even makes sense? In my view it does not and is either a contradiction or mere nonsense.

Bishop Anselm sought to define God's perfection as "that than which nothing greater (or better) can be conceived." In other words, the divine worth is *in all respects* strictly unsurpassable, incapable of growth as well as of rivalry by another. The words are smoothly uttered; but do they convey a clear and consistent idea? Consider the phrase 'greatest possible number.' It, too, can be smoothly uttered, but does it say anything? It might be used to define infinity; but I am not aware of any mathematician who has thought this a good definition. There are in standard mathematics many infinities unequal to one another, but no highest infinity. "Infinite" was a favorite word among classical theists; but they cannot be said to have explored with due care its possible meanings. In any case "not finite" is a negation, and the significance of the negative depends on that of the positive which is negated. If being finite is in every sense a defect, something objectionable, then did not God in creating a world of finite things act objectionably? This seems to me to follow.

Do or do not finite things contribute something to the greatness of God? If so, then each such contribution is itself finite. Does this not mean that somehow finitude has a valid application to the divine life? Consider that, according to the tradition, God could have refrained from creating our world. Then whatever, if anything, this world contributes to the divine life would have been lacking. Moreover, if God could have created some other world instead of this one, God must actually lack what the other world would have contributed. If you reply that the world contributes nothing to the greatness of God, then I ask, What are we all doing, and why talk about "serving God," who, you say, gains nothing whatever from our existence?

The simple conclusion from the foregoing, and still other lines of reasoning, is that the traditional idea of divine perfection or infinity is hopelessly unclear or ambiguous and that persisting in that tradition is bound to cause increasing skepticism, confusion, and human suffering. It has long bred, and must evermore breed, atheism as a natural reaction.

It is only fair to the founders of our religious tradition to remember that their Greek philosophical teachers who inclined to think of deity as wholly unchanging also greatly exaggerated the lack of novelty in many nondivine things. The heavenly bodies were unborn and undying, and changed only by moving in circles; species were fixed forever; the Greek atomists or materialists thought that atoms changed only by altering their positions. Heraclitus, it is true, hinted at a far more basic role for change, and Plato partly followed him. Plato's World Soul, best interpreted as an aspect of God, was not purely eternal, but in its temporal dimension "a moving image of eternity." However, Aristotle, in his view of divinity at least, was more of an eternalist even than Plato, and medieval thought was influenced by Aristotle, also by Philo Judaeus and Plotinus, who likewise stressed the eternalistic side of Plato. Today science and philosophy recognize none of the absolute worldly fixities the Greeks assumed—not the stars, not the species, not the atoms. It more and more appears that creative becoming is no secondary, deficient form of reality compared to being, but is, as Bergson says, "reality itself." Mere being is only an abstraction. Then is there no permanence, does "everything change"? On the contrary (see later, under topic 5), past actualities are permanent. My childhood experiences will be changelessly there in reality, just as they occurred. Change is not finally analyzable as destruction, but only as creation of novelty. The old endures, the new is added.

There are two senses in which freedom from faults, defects, or objectional features, and perfection in *that* sense, may be applied theologically. The divine, to be worthy of worship, must excel any

conceivable being other than itself; it must be unsurpassable *by another*, exalted beyond all possible rivals. Hence all may worship God as in principle forever superior to any other being. This exaltation beyond possible rivals applies to both of the two senses of perfection that I have in mind. There are two kinds (or norms) of excellence, which differ as follows. With one kind it makes sense to talk of an absolute excellence, unsurpassable not only by another being but also by the being itself. This is what the tradition had in mind; and there was in it an important half truth. The neglected other truth, however, is that an absolute best, unsurpassable not only by others but by the being itself, is conceivable only in certain *abstract* aspects of value or greatness, not in fully concrete value or greatness. And God, I hold, is no mere abstraction.

The abstract aspects of value capable of an absolute maximum are goodness and wisdom, or what ought to be meant by the infallibility, righteousness, or holiness of God (one attribute variously expressed). We should conceive the divine knowledge of the world and divine decision-making about it as forever incapable of rivalry and in its infallible rightness incapable of growth. God is not first more or less wicked or foolish (or, like the lower animals, amoral, unaware of ethical principles) and then righteous and wise, but is always beyond criticism in these abstract respects, always wholly wise and good in relating to the world. It is not in such attributes that God can grow. This is so because goodness and rightness are abstract, in a sense in which some values are not.

Put a man in prison. He is not thereby necessarily forced to entertain wrong beliefs, lose virtue, or make wrong decisions. What he is forced to lose is, the aesthetic richness and variety of his impressions. He cannot in the same degree continue to enjoy the beauty of the world. Similarly, a person suffering as Job did is not a happy person, but is not necessarily less virtuous than before. We can go further: ethical goodness and infallibility in knowledge have an upper or absolute limit. Whatever the world may be, God can know without error or ignorance what that world is and can respond to it, taking fully into account the actual and potential values which it involves, and thus be wholly righteous. But if the world first lacks and then acquires new harmonies, new forms of aesthetic richness, then the beauty of the world as divinely known increases. God would be defective in aesthetic capacity were the divine enjoyment not to increase in such a case. Aesthetic value is the most concrete form of value. Everything can contribute to and increase it. *An absolute maximum of beauty is a meaningless idea.* Leibniz tried to define it. Who dares to say that he succeeded? Beauty is unity in variety of experiences. Absolute unity in absolute variety has no clear meaning. Either God lacks any aesthetic sense and then we surpass God in that respect, or there is no upper limit to the divine enjoyment of the beauty of the world.

Plato viewed God as the divine artist, Charles Peirce and A. N. Whitehead termed God the poet of the world. Is the artist not to enjoy the divine work of art, the poet not to enjoy the divine poem? The Hindus attributed bliss to the supreme reality, and many Western theologians have spoken of the divine happiness, but a careful inquiry into the possibility of an absolute upper limit of happiness has not commonly been undertaken. Plato did write about "absolute beauty" but failed to give even a slightly convincing reason for thinking that the phrase has a coherent meaning.

It is not a defect of a Mozart symphony that it lacks the precise form of beauty which a Bach composition has. Aesthetic limitations are not mere defects. The most concrete form of value has no upper limit; there can always be additional values. God can enjoy all the beauty of the actual world and its predecessors, but creativity is inexhaustible and no actual creation can render further creation superfluous. Absolute beauty is a will-o-the-wisp, the search for which has misled multitudes. This is the very rationale of becoming, the reason why mere static being is not enough. Any actual being is less than there could be. There could be more, let there be more. To suppose that this has no application to God is to throw away such clues to value as we have, turn out the light, and use mere words to try to illuminate the darkness that is left.

Two Meanings of "All-Powerful." The idea of omnipotence in the sense to be criticized came about as follows: to be God, that is, worthy of worship, God must in power excel all others (and be open to criticism by none). The highest conceivable form of power must be the divine power. So far so good. Next question: what is the highest conceivable form of power? This question was scarcely

put seriously at all, the answer was felt to be so obvious: it must be the power to determine every detail of what happens in the world. Not, notice, to significantly influence the happenings; no, rather to strictly determine, decide, their every detail. Hence it is that people still today ask, when catastrophe strikes, Why did God do this to me? What mysterious divine reason could there be? Why me? I charge theologians with responsibility for this improper and really absurd question.

Without telling themselves so, the founders of the theological tradition were accepting and applying to deity the *tyrant* ideal of power. "I decide and determine everything, you (and your friends and enemies) merely do what I determine you (and them) to do. Your decision is simply mine for you. You only think you decide: in reality the decision is mine."

Since the theologians were bright people we must not oversimplify. They half-realized they were in trouble. Like many a politician, they indulged in double-talk to hide their mistake even from themselves. They knew they had to define sin as freely deciding to do evil or the lesser good, and as disobeying the will of God. How could one disobey an omnipotent will? There were two devices. One was to say that God does not decide to bring about a sinful act; rather, God decides not to prevent it. God "permits" sin to take place. Taking advantage of this decision, the sinner does his deed. Yet stop! Remember that God is supposed to decide *exactly* what happens in the world. If someone murders me, God has decided there shall be precisely that murderous action. So it turns out that "permits" has here a meaning it ordinarily does not have. Ordinarily, when X gives Y permission to do such and such, there are at least details in the actual doing that are not specified by X (and could not be specified, since human language can give only outlines, not full details, of concrete occurrences). But omnipotence is defined as power to absolutely determine what happens. I have Thomas Aquinas especially in mind here. God gives a creature permission to perform act A, where A is no mere outline but is the act itself in its full concreteness. So nothing at all is left for the creature to decide? What then is left of creaturely freedom?

The most famous of all the scholastics finds the answer, and this is the second of the two devices referred to above. God decides that the creature shall perform act A, but the divine decision is that nevertheless the act shall be performed "freely." Don't laugh, the saintly theologian is serious. Serious, but engaging in doubletalk. It is determined exactly what the creature will do, but determined that he or she will do it freely. As the gangsters sometimes say, after specifying what is to be done, "You are going to like it,"—in other words, to do it with a will. If this is not the despot's ideal of power, what is?

What, let us ask again, is the highest conceivable form of power? Is it the despot's, magnified to infinity, and by hook or crook somehow reconciled with "benevolence," also magnified to infinity? This seems to have been the (partly unconscious) decision of theologians. Is there no better way? Of course there is.

After all, the New Testament analogy—found also in Greek religions—for deity is the parental role, except that in those days of unchallenged male chauvinism it had to be the father role. What is the ideal parental role? Is it that every detail is to be decided by the parent? The question answers itself. The ideal is that the child shall more and more decide its own behavior as its intelligence grows. Wise parents do not try to determine everything, even for the infant, must less for the half-matured or fully matured offspring. Those who do not understand this, and their victims, are among the ones who write agonized letters to Ann Landers. In trying to conceive God, are we to forget everything we know about values? To read some philosophers or theologians it almost seems so.

If the parent does not decide everything, there will be some risk of conflict and frustration in the result. The children are not infallibly wise and good. And indeed, as we shall argue later, even divine wisdom cannot completely foresee (or timelessly know) what others will decide. Life simply is a process of decision making, which means that risk is inherent in life itself. Not even God could make it otherwise. *A world without risks is not conceivable.* At best it would be a totally dead world, with neither good nor evil.

Is it the highest ideal of power to rule over puppets who are permitted to think they make decisions but who are really made by another to do exactly what they do? For twenty centuries we have had theologians who seem to say yes to this question.

creatures as the means, finally, to increase the divine happiness, whose value is no absolute maximum but an ever-enriched infinity.

As a final verbal clarification, I remark that if by 'all-powerful' we mean that God has the highest conceivable form of power and that this power extends to all things—not as, with us, being confined to a tiny corner of the cosmos—and if this is what the word 'omnipotent' can be understood to mean, then yes, God is omnipotent. But the word has been so fearfully misdefined, and has so catastrophically misled so many thinkers, that I incline to say that the word itself had better be dropped. God has power uniquely excellent in quality and scope, in no respect inferior to any coherently conceivable power. In power, as in all properties, God is exalted beyond legitimate criticism or fault finding. In this power I believe. But it is not power to have totally unfree or "absolutely controlled" creatures. For that is nonsense.

Two Meanings of "All-Knowing." The word 'omniscient' seems somewhat less badly tarnished by its historical usage than 'omnipotent.' Whereas having all power (of decision making) would be a monopoly, implying that the creatures had no such power, having all knowledge has no monopolistic implications. Only one agent can genuinely make a certain concrete decision; in contrast, many agents can know one and the same truth, e.g., that two and three is five, or that Julius Caesar was assassinated by Brutus. Hence that God knows all truth is quite compatible with you or your brother knowing many truths.

With omniscience there is one difficulty: either knowing about the future differs essentially from knowing about the past, and hence even God knows our past decisions in one way and knows about the future of our decision making in another way, or else it is merely our human weakness that for us the future is partly indefinite, a matter of what may or may not be, whereas God, exalted altogether beyond such a "limitation," sees the future as completely definite. If God is to be thought in every respect immutable it is this second option that must be taken; but have we any other reason for rejecting the old Socinian proposition that even the highest conceivable form of knowledge is of the past-and-definite *as* past-and-definite and of the future and partly indefinite

as future and partly indefinite? Otherwise would not God be "knowing" the future as what it is not, that is, knowing falsely? As we have seen, the arguments for the complete unchangeability of God are fallacious; hence, the arguments for growth in God's knowledge, as the creative process produces new realities to know, are sound. Thus as Fechner, Berdyaev, Tillich, and, probably independently, Whitehead held (and Berdyaev most neatly formulated), our existence from moment to moment "enriches the divine life." And this is the ultimate meaning of our existence.

Is God all-knowing? Yes, in the Socinian sense. Never has a great intellectual discovery passed with less notice by the world than the Socinian discovery of the proper meaning of omniscience. To this day works of reference fail to tell us about this.

God's Love as Divine Sympathy, Feeling of Others' Feelings. Throughout the Christian centuries there have been a few theologians who have rejected the conception of God as pure intellect or will, as knowing our feelings but feeling nothing, willing our good but not in any intelligible sense *caring* about our pleasures or sufferings. Most theologians rejected feeling as a divine attribute. For them it connoted weakness. True, the Church father Origen said that God felt compassion for humanity and therefore sent the Son as Redeemer. But Origen did not systematically develop the point into a significant philosophical doctrine. In general God was not thought of as sharing our griefs and joys. It was not clear at all that the divine knowledge of our feelings was itself feeling. Fechner, the nineteenth-century psychologist, was perhaps the first great exception to this tradition. The nonconformist English theologian A. E. Garvie was a more recent one. He wrote of the "omnipatience" of God, meaning the divine sympathy with our experiences.

The honor of presenting a worked-out technical philosophical system in which the idea of divine sympathy has its natural place goes to Whitehead, with Fechner the principal anticipator. According to Whitehead, the basic relationship in reality is "prehension," which in the most concrete form (called "physical prehension") is defined as "feeling of feeling," meaning the manner in which one subject feels the feelings of one or more other subjects. In other words, 'sympathy' in the most literal sense. And Whitehead used this word also. Moreover, God is said to know the world by physical prehensions, in other words by feeling the feelings of all the subjects composing that world.

In this philosophy it is not mere benevolence that constitutes the divine nature, it is love in the proper sense. Cruelty to other creatures, or to oneself, means contributing to vicarious divine suffering. Hence, of *course* we should love our fellows as we love ourselves, for the final significance of their joy or sorrow is the same as the final significance of our joy or sorrow, that they will be felt by God. Just so did Fechner see the matter. But the world paid no attention, as it had paid no attention to the Socinian idea of divine knowledge. Merely being right is not enough to impress the busy world, always wrapped up in its more or less unconscious preconceptions. To Whitehead some attention has been paid, but how little compared to the fuss made about Einstein! As Whitehead once remarked to me, Einstein had "all the marks of a great man." Nevertheless, the reason for his fame was not merely the greatness of his discoveries. It was also the fact that they had applications to our physical manipulations of nature, vast industrial and military implications. Theological discoveries are less obvious in their importance.

In fairness to the classical theologians, one thing needs to be said. They realized, quite rightly, that in thinking about God we are likely to apply to deity adjectives that are appropriate enough when applied to ourselves but are unworthy of application to the being exalted above all others, actual or conceivable, and because of this exalted status worthy of being worshiped. To use the word generally employed here, we must in theology beware of *anthropomorphism*, reading our own human traits into our portrait of deity. When theologians read about Jehovah being "angry," they said, "Surely God is above such emotions as anger, along with those of envy, jealousy, and the like!" All these indications of human weakness in the Biblical account of deity were set aside as concessions to the ignorance or innocence of ordinary people, incapable of the refinements of scholarship or philosophy. Human beings are theologically said to be "images of God"; but the danger of underestimating the vast difference between creatures and Creator is obvious. What seems so strange in the traditional, largely Greek,

conception of God adopted in the Dark Ages and kept intact through the Middle Ages and beyond is partly explained by the vigorous and—if kept within its proper limits—justified effort to keep clear of anthropomorphic tarnishing of the description of God. Certainly, a being totally and in every respect immmutable and open to no increase in value is extremely different from ourselves; however, it is far from clear that anything is left of the "image of God" that is supposed to be in us, and that indeed must be in us if we are to have any idea of God.

What it comes to is that in retreating from popular anthropomorphism classical theology fell backward into an opposite error. Intent on not exaggerating the likeness of the divine and the human, they did away with it altogether, if one takes their statements literally. Using the word 'love', they emptied it of its most essential kernel, the element of sympathy, of the feeling of others' feelings. It became mere beneficence, totally unmoved (to use their own word) by the sufferings or joys of the creatures. Who wants a friend who loves only in that sense? A heartless benefit machine is less than a friend.

If anyone has been more learned in medieval thought than the Jewish scholar Harry Wolfson I have not learned his name. Wolfson's considered judgment was that the scholastic theology utterly failed to express the Biblical idea of God. Many Christian scholars, including the father of the author of this book, have agreed with Wolfson. Many more-or-less skeptical or agnostic philosophers have also agreed with the judgment. A well-meaning attempt to purify theology of anthropomorphism purified it of any genuine, consistent meaning at all. After all, the problem of anthropomorphism is not so simple that only one kind of mistake can be made in dealing with it. If an anthropomorphic idea is one that expresses our human nature, in what sense can we have a nonanthropomorphic idea? Said Emerson, "All of the thoughts of a turtle are turtle." Is it any less true that all of a human being's thoughts are human?

Human beings, unlike turtles, have not only ideas but ideas about ideas. We can make of abstractions things to talk about. If our ideas are all human, we are the ones who can say that this is so. Can the turtle say or in any way think the corresponding thought about itself? Probably not. What is the moral? Charles Peirce a fearful burden on our democracy. It was not an accident that the founders of our republic were far from fundamentalist Christians. Jefferson, Franklin, Ethan Allen, Lincoln, and still others were believers in God but not in the infallibility of any book or human institution. The same is true of Emerson, our great poet whose prose was more poetic than most verse. It holds also for Peirce, James, and Royce, three of our greatest philosophers. Is it desirable that religion should seem more and more an affair of the intellectually undistinguished or mediocre?

The Principle of Dual Transcendence

The first four of the mistakes dealt with above are "one-sided" views in that they seek to distinguish God from all else by putting God on one side of a long list of contraries: finite-infinite, temporal-eternal, relative-absolute, contingent-necessary, physical-spiritual, and still others. But this is a species of idolatry, implying that what we worship is infinity, eternity, absoluteness, necessity, mere spirituality, or disembodied mind. But these are empty abstractions. So is love, if you only mean the mere quality of lovingness. What is really worshipful is the love which is infinite in whatever sense that is an excellence and is finite in whatever sense that, too, is an excellence. God contrasts with creatures, not as infinite with finite, but as *infinite-and-finite (both in uniquely excellent ways*, beyond all possible rivalry or relevant criticism) contrasts with the merely fragmentary and only surpassably excellent creatures. God contrasts with creatures, not as the merely absolute contrasts with the relative, but as the absolute-and-relative in uniquely excellent ways contrasts with the creatures as neither relative nor absolute, except in senses in which they are surpassable by others. God is similarly both eternal and temporal in all-surpassing ways; God alone has an *eternal individuality*, meaning unborn and undying, and God alone has enjoyed the entire past and will enjoy all the future. He-She is both physical and spiritual, and the divine body (see the next chapter) is all-surpassing and all-inclusive of the creaturely bodies, which are to God as cells to a supercellular organism. His-Her

spirit embraces all the psychical there is with all-surpassing, unstinted love.

The idea of omnipotence, as usually construed, contradicts dual transcendence; for it means that God is wholly active, independent, or absolute in relation to the creatures and that the creatures are wholly passive in relation to God. It means that God does either everything or nothing. If everything, then the creatures do nothing and are nothing. The divine excellence is a uniquely excellent way of interacting with others, of being active *and* passive in relation to them. We do things to God by deciding our own being, with necessary help from God, as setting limits to the disorder inherent in freedom, and as inspiring us to take our place in the cosmic order as best we can. God loves us as we partly make ourselves to be, not simply as we are divinely made to be. To say that a lover is uninfluenced by a partly self-made loved one is nonsense or contradiction. Omnipotence was often taken in a way that amounts to that contradiction.

The formula "dual transcendence" is mine. The basic idea is in Whitehead and still others, but in some respects less sharply formulated. The criticism, made for instance by a conservative English theologian, that it is contradictory to attribute both finitude and infinity, for example, to the same deity is nothing but the neglect of an elementary logical truth, which is that the description of something as both P and not-P (where P is some predicate or property) is contradictory *only* if the predicate and its negation are applied in "the same respect" to the something in question. And dual transcendence does not make or permit such an application. Moreover, it offers a definite explanation of how the difference in the two respects is possible. The absolute, infinite side is abstract and concerns the divine potentiality or capacity to have values, while the finitude or relativity concerns the divine actuality. If you or I had made different decisions, God would have enjoyed (or suffered) these other decisions. Anything that could be actual God could divinely have, but what God actually has depends partly on creaturely decisions. This is the social structure of existence. The primacy of love means that there is no possible value that any being could have simply in and by itself, or simply by its own decision.

Aristotle said that the abstract or universal is real only in the concrete and individual. But he failed to realize how abstract and merely universal was his idea of God, defined as unmoved mover changelessly thinking—thinking what? The divine thinking, Aristotle said, was simply thinking thinking itself. Particular things or individuals, such as you or me, are not worth knowing about. Only eternal essences, universals, are worth knowing. And so if we know both the universal essence human, and this or that particular human person, we know what God does and something more besides. The Greek fascination with abstractions and disparagement of the concrete could not have been better displayed than in this paradox. Of course few theologians, least of all Christian theologians, could so disparage the worth of individuals when even a sparrow is said in the Gospels to be of interest to the Heavenly Father. But the theologians failed, on their part, to realize what Aristotle had seen very clearly, that if, contrary to Aristotle's opinion, God is aware of particular individuals and their careers, then the entire fullness of reality must be embraced in divine knowledge. But this concrete fullness is not eternal, it receives new items moment by moment. Also some at least of the items are contingent, results of free decisions, divine or creaturely, or both. Hence it will no longer do to hold that God is exclusively eternal and necessary, rather than also temporal and contingent. Like it or not, the door to the doctrine of dual transcendence has been opened.

We do not contradict ourselves if we say that a certain person is unchanging in being always (reasonably) "kind," although of course in concrete particulars responding differently to take changing circumstances into account. The idealized form of this contrast can be applied to God, who alone can unfailingly conform to the ideal of kindness.

That there are really different aspects of the divine nature, as dual transcendence implies, will be rejected by some thinkers on the ground that God is "simple," a traditional doctrine. But as used against dual transcendence, this argument would be purely question-begging. God is both simple and complex, the one in abstract, the other in concrete aspects. For instance, the divine cognitive infallibility is not really different (illustrating simplicity) from the divine ethical infallibility. But the aesthetic value actualized

in God is no mere infallibility of the divine aesthetic capacity to respond. Aesthetic value, unlike merely cognitive or ethical value, depends in part upon what is responded to. It is concrete. There is a real difference (illustrating complexity) between the absolutely unsurpassable cognitive perfection of God's knowing, or the absolute rightness of the divine decision-making about the creatures, and the beauty of the actual, cosmic poem (the "verses" of which are partly self-decided) as divinely enjoyed.

Paul Tillich's "God is being but not *a* being," that is, universal but not individual, violates dual transcendence and is open to the objections to be made against all such violations, that they either make God an empty abstraction, or else make Him-Her a fetish, a *merely* finite, relative, and changeable individual . A merely finite God of course will not do. The only infinity some of us can see as making sense we do attribute to God, but not the meaningless, contradictory, or empty *mere* infinity of the traditional view.

Since the fifth and sixth mistakes are not about the uniquely exalted nature or function of God but about the special nature or status of our human species, dual transcendence does not apply to these latter topics—unless our species is indeed transcendent, an infinite exception in nature, supernatural in the sense in which God is. And that is precisely the issue between the traditional view and the new view of immortality. Like all animals we have finite careers between birth and death; but the old view of immortality holds that we have infinite careers after death. This is an extreme view. The opposite extreme is that after death our careers become less than finite, they become reduced to zero. As corpses we have no sequence of live experiences, finite or infinite. We are dead and unconscious. What was something is now nothing. Yet how can the same reality be both something and nothing? The modest but positive view of immortality is that our years of aliveness will always be just that.

Ask yourself, what is Julius Caesar now? That Caesar is "not now alive" means that while Caesar's experience and action are still having influence on our present world and ourselves, we and our world are having no influence on Caesar. Our contemporaries are those we can interact with; our ancestors still do things to us, but never can we do anything to them. This is the meaning of the

BOOK II

Adolescence

i (1)   I intend to remind myself of my past foulnesses and carnal corruptions, not because I love them but so that I may love you, my God. It is from love of your love that I make the act of recollection. The recalling of my wicked ways is bitter in my memory, but I do it so that you may be sweet to me, a sweetness touched by no deception, a sweetness serene and content. You gathered me together from the state of disintegration in which I had been fruitlessly divided. I turned from unity in you to be lost in multiplicity.[1]

At one time in adolescence I was burning to find satisfaction in hellish pleasures. I ran wild in the shadowy jungle of erotic adventures. 'My beauty wasted away and in your sight I became putrid' (Dan. 10: 8), by pleasing myself and by being ambitious to win human approval.

ii (2)   The single desire that dominated my search for delight was simply to love and to be loved. But no restraint was imposed by the exchange of mind with mind, which marks the brightly lit pathway of friendship. Clouds of muddy carnal concupiscence filled the air. The bubbling impulses of puberty befogged and obscured my heart so that it could not see the difference between love's serenity and lust's darkness. Confusion of the two things boiled within me. It seized hold of my youthful weakness sweeping me through the precipitous rocks of desire to submerge me in a whirlpool of vice.[2] Your wrath was heavy upon me and I was unaware of it. I had become deafened by the clanking chain[3] of my mortal condition, the penalty of my pride. I travelled very far from you, and you did not stop me. I was tossed about and spilt, scattered and boiled dry in my fornications. And you were silent. How slow I was to find my joy! At that time you said nothing, and I travelled much further away from

---

[1] The language here is characteristic of Porphyry (e.g. *ep. ad Marcellam* 10, p. 280, 25 Nauck) and Plotinus 6. 6. 1. 5. See below XI. xxix (39).

[2] Echo of Virgil, *Aeneid* 3. 422 (Scylla and Charybdis).

[3] Virgil, *Aeneid* 6. 558.

you into more and more sterile things productive of unhappiness, proud in my self-pity, incapable of rest in my exhaustion.

(3)   If only someone could have imposed restraint on my disorder. That would have transformed to good purpose the fleeting experiences of beauty in these lowest of things, and fixed limits to indulgence in their charms. Then the stormy waves of my youth would have finally broken on the shore of marriage. Even so, I could not have been wholly content to confine sexual union to acts intended to procreate children, as your law prescribes, Lord. For you shape the propagation of our mortal race, imposing your gentle hand to soften the brambles which were excluded from your paradise.[4] Your omnipotence is never far from us, even when we are far from you.[5] Alternatively, I ought to have paid more vigilant heed to the voice from your clouds: 'Nevertheless those who are married shall have trouble in the flesh, and I would spare you' (Cor. 7: 28), and 'It is good for a man not to touch a woman' (1 Cor. 7: 1), and 'He who has no wife thinks on the things of God, how he can please God. But he who is joined in marriage thinks on the affairs of the world, how he can please his wife' (1 Cor. 7: 32–3). Had I paid careful attention to these sayings and 'become a eunuch for the sake of the kingdom of heaven' (Matt. 19: 12), I would have been happier finding fulfilment in your embraces.

(4)   But I in my misery seethed and followed the driving force of my impulses, abandoning you. I exceeded all the bounds set by your law, and did not escape your chastisement—indeed no mortal can do so. For you were always with me, mercifully punishing me, touching with a bitter taste all my illicit pleasures. Your intention was that I should seek delights unspoilt by disgust and that, in my quest where I could achieve this, I should discover it to be in nothing except you Lord, nothing but you. You 'fashion pain to be a lesson' (Ps. 93: 20 LXX), you 'strike to heal', you bring death upon us so that we should not die apart from you (Deut. 32: 39).[6]

---

[4] Augustine's vision of the sex-life of Adam and Eve before the Fall passed from belief that their union was wholly spiritual (below XIII. xx (28)) to a conviction that it was both spiritual and physical, but controlled by reason and will, never by unreasoning passion, and wholly free of the thorny problems that beset sexuality in common experience.

[5] The Neoplatonist Porphyry wrote: 'He who knows God has God present to him, and he who does not know him is absent from him who is everywhere present.' (*Ad Gaurum* 12. 3). Cf. above, II. ii (3).

[6] Cf. above I. v. (6). The beneficence of punishment is affirmed in 2 Macc. 6: 12–16.

Where was I in the sixteenth year of the age of my flesh? 'Far away in exile from the pleasures of your house' (Mic. 2: 9). Sensual folly assumed domination over me, and I gave myself totally to it in acts allowed by shameful humanity but under your laws illicit. My family did not try to extricate me from my headlong course by means of marriage. The only concern was that I should learn to speak as effectively as possible and carry conviction by my oratory.

iii (5)   During my sixteenth year there was an interruption in my studies. I was recalled from Madauros, the nearby town where I had first lived away from home to learn literature and oratory. During that time funds were gathered in preparation for a more distant absence at Carthage, for which my father had more enthusiasm than cash, since he was a citizen of Thagaste with very modest resources.[7] To whom do I tell these things? Not to you, my God. But before you I declare this to my race, to the human race, though only a tiny part can light on this composition of mine. And why do I include this episode? It is that I and any of my readers may reflect on the great depth from which we have to cry to you (Ps. 129: 1). Nothing is nearer to your ears than a confessing heart and a life grounded in faith (cf. Rom. 10: 9). At that time everybody was full of praise for my father because he spent money on his son beyond the means of his estate, when that was necessary to finance an education entailing a long journey. Many citizens of far greater wealth did nothing of the kind for their children. But this same father did not care what character before you I was developing, or how chaste I was so long as I possessed a cultured tongue—though my culture really meant a desert uncultivated by you, God. You are the one true and good lord of your land, which is my heart.

(6)   In my sixteenth year idleness interposed because of my family's lack of funds. I was on holiday from all schooling and lived with my parents. The thorns of lust rose above my head, and there was no hand to root them out. Indeed, when at the bathhouse my father saw that I was showing signs of virility and the stirrings of adolescence,

---

[7] Augustine's biographer, Possidius, records that his father Patrick sat on the town council or *curia* of Thagaste, a position bringing social credit and financial burdens. The estate was not large, and in relative terms the family was reckoned 'poor', i.e. it possessed only a few slaves for the housework and the land, which in one letter Augustine describes as 'a few acres'. Naturally Augustine's family was not poor in an absolute sense; they were far from being destitute. But 'pauper' is once defined by Ovid as 'a man who knows how many sheep he has'. Patrick is likely to have known how many he had.

he was overjoyed to suppose that he would now be having grand-children, and told my mother so. His delight was that of the intoxication which makes the world oblivious of you, its Creator, and to love your creation instead of you. He was drunk with the invisible wine of his perverse will directed downwards to inferior things.[8] But in my mother's heart you had already begun your temple and the beginning of your holy habitation (Ecclus. 24: 14). My father was still a catechumen and had become that only recently. So she shook with a pious trepidation and a holy fear (2 Cor. 7: 15). For, although I had not yet become a baptized believer, she feared the twisted paths along which walk those who turn their backs and not their face towards you (Jer. 2: 27).

(7)   Wretch that I am, do I dare to say that you, my God, were silent when in reality I was travelling farther from you? Was it in this sense that you kept silence to me? Then whose words were they but yours which you were chanting in my ears through my mother, your faithful servant? But nothing of that went down into my heart to issue in action. Her concern (and in the secret of my conscience I recall the memory of her admonition delivered with vehement anxiety) was that I should not fall into fornication, and above all that I should not commit adultery with someone else's wife. These warnings seemed to me womanish advice which I would have blushed to take the least notice of. But they were your warnings and I did not realize it. I believed you were silent, and that it was only she who was speaking, when you were speaking to me through her. In her you were scorned by me, by me her son, the son of your handmaid, your servant (Ps. 115: 16). But I did not realize this and went on my way headlong with such blindness that among my peer group I was ashamed not to be equally guilty of shameful behaviour when I heard them boasting of their sexual exploits. Their pride was the more aggressive, the more debauched their acts were; they derived pleasure not merely from the lust of the act but also from the admiration it evoked. What is more worthy of censure than vice? Yet I went deeper into vice to avoid being despised, and when there was no act by admitting to which I could rival my depraved companions, I used to pretend I had done things I had not done at

---

[8] Augustine's father celebrated the signs of his son's virility by becoming inebriated. The implications of this passage on Patrick's hopes for a grandchild appear the only evidence to suggest that Augustine was the eldest of the children.

all, so that my innocence should not lead my companions to scorn my lack of courage, and lest my chastity be taken as a mark of inferiority.[9]

(8)   Such were the companions with whom I made my way through the streets of Babylon.[10] With them I rolled in its dung as if rolling in spices and precious ointments (S. of S. 5. 4: 14). To tie me down the more tenaciously to Babylon's belly, the invisible enemy trampled on me (Ps. 55: 3) and seduced me because I was in the mood to be seduced. The mother of my flesh already had fled from the centre of Babylon (Jer. 51: 6), but still lingered in the outskirts of the city. Although she had warned me to guard my virginity, she did not seriously pay heed to what her husband had told her about me, and which she felt to hold danger for the future: for she did not seek to restrain my sexual drive within the limit of the marriage bond, if it could not be cut back to the quick. The reason why she showed no such concern was that she was afraid that the hope she placed in me could be impeded by a wife. This was not the hope which my mother placed in you for the life to come, but the hope which my parents entertained for my career that I might do well out of the study of literature. Both of them, as I realized, were very ambitious for me: my father because he hardly gave a thought to you at all, and his ambitions for me were concerned with mere vanities; my mother because she thought it would do no harm and would be a help to set me on the way towards you, if I studied the traditional pattern of a literary education. That at least is my conjecture as I try to recall the characters of my parents.

The reins were relaxed to allow me to amuse myself. There was no strict discipline to keep me in check, which led to an unbridled dissoluteness in many different directions. In all of this there was a thick mist shutting me off from the brightness of your face, my God, and my iniquity as it were 'burst out from my fatness' (Ps. 72: 7).

iv (9)   Theft receives certain punishment by your law (Exod. 20: 15), Lord, and by the law written in the hearts of men (Rom. 2: 14) which not even iniquity itself destroys. For what thief can with

---

[9] The theme of this paragraph is found in Ambrose, *Noah* 22, 81.

[10] Augustine's portrait of his wild years may be compared with the savage contemporary portrait of the riff-raff of Rome about 380 by the pagan historian Ammianus Marcellinus, who speaks of people spending their entire lives on alcohol, gambling, brothels, and public shows (28. 4. 28).

equanimity endure being robbed by another thief? He cannot tolerate it even if he is rich and the other is destitute. I wanted to carry out an act of theft and did so, driven by no kind of need other than my inner lack of any sense of, or feeling for, justice. Wickedness filled me. I stole something which I had in plenty and of much better quality. My desire was to enjoy not what I sought by stealing but merely the excitement of thieving and the doing of what was wrong. There was a pear tree near our vineyard laden with fruit, though attractive in neither colour nor taste. To shake the fruit off the tree and carry off the pears, I and a gang of naughty adolescents set off late at night after (in our usual pestilential way) we had continued our game in the streets. We carried off a huge load of pears. But they were not for our feasts but merely to throw to the pigs. Even if we ate a few, nevertheless our pleasure lay in doing what was not allowed.

Such was my heart, O God, such was my heart. You had pity on it when it was at the bottom of the abyss. Now let my heart tell you what it was seeking there in that I became evil for no reason.[11] I had no motive for my wickedness except wickedness itself. It was foul, and I loved it. I loved the self-destruction, I loved my fall, not the object for which I had fallen but my fall itself. My depraved soul leaped down from your firmament to ruin.[12] I was seeking not to gain anything by shameful means, but shame for its own sake.

v (10) There is beauty in lovely physical objects, as in gold and silver and all other such things. When the body touches such things, much significance attaches to the rapport of the object with the touch. Each of the other senses has its own appropriate mode of response to physical things. Temporal honour and the power of giving orders and of being in command have their own kind of dignity, though this is also the origin of the urge to self-assertion. Yet in the acquisition of all these sources of social status, one must not depart from you, Lord, nor deviate from your law. The life which we live in this world has its attractiveness because of a certain measure in its beauty and its harmony with all these inferior objects that are beautiful. Human friendship is also a nest of love and gentleness because of the unity it brings about between

[11] Echo of Sallust's language about Catiline. Augustine presents himself as a new Catiline.

[12] Like Lucifer.

many souls. Yet sin is committed for the sake of all these things and others of this kind when, in consequence of an immoderate urge towards those things which are at the bottom end of the scale of good,[13] we abandon the higher and supreme goods, that is you, Lord God, and your truth and your law (Ps. 118: 142). These inferior goods have their delights, but not comparable to my God who has made them all. It is in him that the just person takes delight; he is the joy of those who are true of heart (Ps. 63: 11).

(11)   When a crime is under investigation to discover the motive for which it was done, the accusation is not usually believed except in cases where the appetite to obtain (or the fear of losing) one of those goods which we have called inferior appears a plausible possibility. They are beautiful and attractive even if, in comparison with the higher goods which give true happiness, they are mean and base. A man committed murder. Why? Because he loved another's wife or his property; or he wanted to acquire money to live on by plundering his goods; or he was afraid of losing his own property by the action of his victim; or he had suffered injury and burned with desire for revenge. No one would commit murder without a motive, merely because he took pleasure in killing. Who would believe that? It was said of one brutal and cruel man [Catiline] that he was evil and savage without reason.[14] Yet the preceding passage gave the motive: 'lest disuse might make his hand or mind slow to react'. Why did he wish for that? Why so? His objective was to capture the city by violent crimes to obtain honours, government, and wealth; to live without fear of the laws and without the difficulty of attaining his ambitions because of the poverty of his family estate and his known criminal record. No, not even Catiline himself loved his crimes; something else motivated him to commit them.

vi (12)   Wretch that I was, what did I love in you, my act of theft, that crime which I did at night in the sixteenth year of my life? There was nothing beautiful about you, my thieving. Indeed do you exist at all for me to be addressing you?

    The fruit which we stole was beautiful because it was your creation, most beautiful of all Beings, maker of all things, the good

---

[13] Throughout his writings Augustine holds to a doctrine of gradations of goodness. The good of the body is inferior to that of the soul; the will, in itself midway, may turn to higher or to lower things, and may err by preferring inferior goods to superior.

[14] Sallust, *Catiline* 16 (also cited by Augustine, *Sermon on Ps. 108*, 3).

God, God the highest good and my true good. The fruit was beautiful, but was not that which my miserable soul coveted. I had a quantity of better pears. But those I picked solely with the motive of stealing. I threw away what I had picked. My feasting was only on the wickedness which I took pleasure in enjoying. If any of those pears entered my mouth, my criminality was the piquant sauce. And now, Lord my God, I inquire what was the nature of my pleasure in the theft. The act has nothing lovely about it, none of the loveliness found in equity and prudence, or in the human mind whether in the memory or in the senses or in physical vitality. Nor was it beautiful in the way the stars are, noble in their courses, or earth and sea full of newborn creatures which, as they are born, take the place of those which die;[15] not even in the way that specious vices have a flawed reflection of beauty.

(13) Pride imitates what is lofty; but you alone are God most high above all things. What does ambition seek but honour and glory? Yet you alone are worthy of honour and are glorious for eternity. The cruelty of powerful people aims to arouse fear. Who is to be feared but God alone? What can be seized or stolen from his power? When or where or how or by whom? Soft endearments are intended to arouse love. But there are no caresses tenderer than your charity, and no object of love is more healthy than your truth, beautiful and luminous beyond all things. Curiosity appears to be a zeal for knowledge; yet you supremely know all. Ignorance and stupidity are given the names of simplicity and innocence; but there is no greater simplicity than in you. And what greater innocence than yours, whereas to evil men their own works are damaging? Idleness appears as desire for a quiet life; yet can rest be assured apart from the Lord? Luxury wants to be called abundance and satiety; but you are fullness and the inexhaustible treasure of incorruptible pleasure. Prodigality presents itself under the shadow of generosity; but you are the rich bestower of all good things. Avarice wishes to have large possessions; you possess everything. Envy contends about excellence; but what is more excellent than you? Anger seeks revenge; who avenges with greater justice than you? Fear quails before sudden and unexpected events attacking things which are

---

[15] Augustine regarded the cycle of birth and death as 'beautiful'; i.e. death is evil to the individual, not to the race.

loved, and takes precautions for their safety; to you is anything unexpected or sudden? Or who can take away from you what you love? There is no reliable security except with you. Regret wastes away for the loss of things which cupidity delighted in. Its wish would be that nothing be taken away, just as nothing can be taken from you.

(14)   So the soul fornicates (Ps. 72: 27) when it is turned away from you and seeks outside you the pure and clear intentions which are not to be found except by returning to you. In their perverted way all humanity imitates you. Yet they put themselves at a distance from you and exalt themselves against you. But even by thus imitating you they acknowledge that you are the creator of all nature and so concede that there is no place where one can entirely escape from you. Therefore in that act of theft what was the object of my love, and in what way did I viciously and perversely imitate my Lord? Was my pleasure to break your law, but by deceit since I had not the power to do that by force? Was I acting like a prisoner with restricted liberty who does without punishment what is not permitted, thereby making an assertion of possessing a dim resemblance to omnipotence? Here is a runaway slave fleeing his master and pursuing a shadow (Job 7: 2). What rottenness! What a monstrous life and what an abyss of death! Was it possible to take pleasure in what was illicit for no reason other than that it was not allowed?

vii (15)   'What shall I render to the Lord?' (Ps. 115: 2) who recalls these things to my memory, but my soul feels no fear from the recollection. I will love you, Lord, and I will give thanks and confession to your name because you have forgiven me such great evils and my nefarious deeds. I attribute to your grace and mercy that you have melted my sins away like ice (Ecclus. 3: 17). I also attribute to your grace whatever evil acts I have not done. What could I not have done when I loved gratuitous crime? I confess that everything has been forgiven, both the evil things I did of my own accord, and those which I did not do because of your guidance.

No one who considers his frailty would dare to attribute to his own strength his chastity and innocence, so that he has less cause to love you—as if he had less need of your mercy by which you forgive the sins of those converted to you. If man is called by you, follows your voice, and has avoided doing those acts which I am recalling and avowing in my own life, he should not mock the healing of a sick man by the Physician, whose help has kept him from falling sick, or at least enabled him to be less gravely ill. He should love you no less, indeed even more; for he sees that the one who delivered me from the great sicknesses of my sins is also he through whom he may see that he himself has not been a victim of the same great sicknesses.

viii (16) 'What fruit had I', wretched boy, in these things (Rom. 6: 21) which I now blush to recall, above all in that theft in which I loved nothing but the theft itself? The theft itself was a nothing, and for that reason I was the more miserable. Yet had I been alone I would not have done it—I remember my state of mind to be thus at the time—alone I would never have done it. Therefore my love in that act was to be associated with the gang in whose company I did it. Does it follow that I loved something other than the theft? No, nothing else in reality because association with the gang is also a nothing. What is it in reality? Who can teach me that, but he who 'illuminates my heart' (Ecclus. 2: 10) and disperses the shadows in it? What else has stirred my mind to ask and discuss and consider this question? If I had liked the pears which I stole and actually desired to enjoy them, I could by myself have committed that wicked act, had it been enough to attain the pleasure which I sought. I would not have needed to inflame the itch of my cupidity through the excitement generated by sharing the guilt with others. But my pleasure was not in the pears; it was in the crime itself, done in association with a sinful group.

ix (17) What was my state of mind? It is quite certain that it was utterly shameful and a disgrace to me that I had it. Yet what was it? 'Who understands his sins?' (Job 10: 15). It was all done for a giggle, as if our hearts were tickled to think we were deceiving those who would not think us capable of such behaviour and would have profoundly disapproved. Why then did I derive pleasure from an act I would not have done on my own? Is it that nobody can easily laugh when alone? Certainly no one readily laughs when alone; yet sometimes laughter overcomes individuals when no one else is present if their senses or their mind perceive something utterly absurd. But alone I would not have done it, could not conceivably have done it by myself. See, before you, my God, the living memory of

48

my soul. Alone I would not have committed that crime, in which my pleasure lay not in what I was stealing but in the act of theft. But had I been alone, it would have given me absolutely no pleasure, nor would I have committed it. Friendship can be a dangerous enemy, a seduction of the mind lying beyond the reach of investigation.[16] Out of a game and a jest came an avid desire to do injury and an appetite to inflict loss on someone else without any motive on my part of personal gain, and no pleasure in settling a score. As soon as the words are spoken 'Let us go and do it', one is ashamed not to be shameless.

x (18)   Who can untie this extremely twisted and tangled knot? It is a foul affair, I have no wish to give attention to it; I have no desire to contemplate it. My desire is for you, justice and innocence, you are lovely and splendid to honest eyes; the satiety of your love is insatiable. With you is utter peace and a life immune from disturbance. The person who enters into you 'enters into the joy of the Lord' (Matt. 25: 21), and will not be afraid; he will find himself in the supreme Good where it is supremely good to be. As an adolescent I went astray from you (Ps. 118: 76), my God, far from your unmoved stability. I became to myself a region of destitution.[17]

---

[16] Similarly IX. ii. (2).

[17] The Prodigal Son is fused with a Neoplatonic theme of the soul's destitution without God, which is taken up at the beginning of book III and again in VII. x (16). Destitution in the soul distant from God is a theme in Porphyry (*De abstinentia* 3. 27 and *Sententiae* 40), based on Plato's *Symposium*.

DOCTRINE: THE REAL ISSUE!

Fundamentalism was born out of a doctrinal controversy with Liberalism. The ultimate issue is whether Christians who have a supernatural religion are going to be overpowered by Christians who have only a humanistic philosophy of life. Fundamentalism is the affirmation of Christian belief and a distinctively Christian life-style as opposed to the general secular society. It is the opposite of radical liberal Protestantism, which has attempted both to secularize Christianity and to Christianize secularism at the same time.[16] Viewed from the standpoint of supernaturalism vs. secularism, Barr is right when he observes that there is ultimately very little difference between the theological framework of Fundamentalists and that of Evangelicals. While acknowledging that a difference of attitude does exist between the two, he nevertheless exposes the Evangelical Movement for attempting to hide its Fundamentalism behind the "conservative Evangelical" label. He asks the rather searching question: "Has Evangelicalism succeeded in developing a conceptual framework recognizable, distinct from the Fundamentalist one?" Then he answers his own question: "It is not clear that modernized and updated Evangelicalism has yet attained to any conceptual framework that is intrinsically different from the

Fundamentalist one, or that it has even tried."[17] This point is exactly what contemporary Evangelicalism needs to face—the fact that it is not intrinsically different from the mainstream of Fundamentalism!

To an outsider such as Barr, Evangelicalism and Fundamentalism seem to be in fact one and the same. While we Americans recognize strong differences between the extremities within the two movements, we too must face the fact that we share a common heritage which goes back to the fundamentalist controversy of the 1920s. The time has come for the Evangelicals to quit pretending that they do not know who we Fundamentalists are and to stop denying their relationship to us. We need to present a unified effort to stand for the basic truths of Scripture that we both hold dear.

Most people trace the basics of Fundamentalism back to the five fundamentals that became crucial in the fundamentalist-modernist controversy. These are usually expressed as:

1. The inspiration and infallibility of Scripture.
2. The deity of Christ (including His virgin birth).
3. The substitutionary atonement of Christ's death.
4. The literal resurrection of Christ from the dead.
5. The literal return of Christ in the Second Advent.

This list of Christian essentials has been expanded and amplified many times, including such issues as the doctrine of the Holy Spirit, the depravity of humankind, belief in a literal heaven and hell, the importance of soul-winning and evangelism, the existence of the person of Satan, and the importance of the local church.[18] Nevertheless, it is more correct to limit the definition of doctrinal Fundamentalism to the essential fundamentals that have been the heart of the movement for nearly a century now.

Inspiration and
Infallibility of Scripture

The fundamentalist position on the inspiration of Scripture is essentially that of the main-line Evangelical Movement.[19] Both groups ultimately go back to the plenary-verbal inspiration concept of Warfield and the Princeton theologians of the nineteenth century. Believing this to be the historical Christian understanding of Scripture, Fundamentalists and Evangelicals alike hold to a basic belief in the inerrancy of the Scriptures in their original autographs. To Fundamentalists, the inerrancy of Scripture is ultimately linked to the legitimacy and authority of the Bible.[20] They view the Bible as being God-breathed and thus possessing the quality of being free from error in all of its statements and affirmations. Robert Lightner asks: "How can an errant Bible be God's revelation? How can it be God-breathed? How can it possibly be authoritative and therefore trustworthy? How can Scripture possibly be inerrant in some parts and errant in others at the same time? In a book which claims God as its author, inspiration must extend to all its parts. If it does not, how does one go about determining what is and what is not God-breathed and therefore free from error?"[21] He rightly observes that the trend among radical Evangelicals away from the total inerrancy of the Scriptures is really nothing more than an intellectual accommodation to contemporary society.

Deity of Christ

The deity of Christ is really the most essential fundamental of all.[22] Attention has shifted in the past decade to the issue of the inspiration of Scripture, since it is from Scripture that Evangelicals derive their basic doctrinal beliefs. Nevertheless, the basic issue that was strongly defended by the early Fundamentalists was the person of Christ. This is evidenced in the article by William G. Moorehead, then president of Xenia Theological Seminary, entitled "The Moral Glory of Jesus Christ, a Proof of Inspiration."[23] Fundamentalists have always felt that belief in the deity of Christ was impugned by a denial of the inspiration of Scripture, since Christ Himself quoted Old Testament Scripture as being inspired of God and even referred to "questionable" individuals as having actually existed (Adam, Jonah, and others). The article on the deity of Christ in *The Fundamentals* was written by Warfield himself. In this article he argued that the proof of the deity of Christ was more than evident in Scripture. Christ Himself claimed to be God, accepted worship from others, and was looked upon as divine by the apostles and the early Church. To this Warfield added the argument of the personal experience of the believer. Though admittedly subjective, Warfield, like all true Christians, announced: "The supreme proof to every Christian of the deity of his Lord is in his own inner experience of the transforming power of his Lord upon the heart and life. Not more surely does he who feels the present warmth of the sun know that the sun exists, than he who has experienced the recreative power of the Lord know Him to be his Lord and his God."[24]

The strength of this argument cannot be underestimated when evaluating the commitment of Bible-believing Christians to the Christ of Scripture. For it goes far beyond their intellectual adherence to the inspiration, infallibility, and inerrancy of Scripture. It is their deep and personal devotion to the person of Jesus Christ Himself that will not enable them ever to let go of the Bible. It is this love for Jesus that drives Fundamentalist-Evangelicals to cling to the truth of Scripture beyond all the rational arguments of all the critics of all of time. This truth has been virtually unobserved because it is not understood by those who do not share it. Evangelical-Fundamentalists will not let go of the Scripture because it is the Scripture that has led them to their personal experiential relationship with the living Christ. For them to deny the Scripture, which brought them to Christ, would be like the scientist denying the formula that proved the results of an experiment.

A related issue is that of the virgin birth of Christ, which Fundamentalists view as having definite implications regarding the doctrine of the deity of Christ. This article in *The Fundamentals* was written by the Scottish theologian Dr. James Orr. To him, and the other Fundamentalists, this was no optional doctrine which had no real significance in relation to the doctrine of the person of Christ. Orr emphatically states: "Doctrinally, it must be repeated that the belief in the Virgin birth of Christ is of the highest value in the right apprehension of Christ's unique and sinless personality."[25]

Substitutionary Atonement

The doctrine of the substitutionary atonement of Christ's death is also intertwined with that of His deity. At the time of the fundamentalist controversy several new theories regarding the atonement of Christ were being propagated relative to the idea of His death being little more than a moral influence on society. To Fundamentalists, this struck at the very heart and core of Christianity. The entire message of the Gospel centers around the death, burial, and resurrection of Christ. If He did not die for sin as God's substitute for man and if He were not literally raised from the dead, then there would be no Good News to proclaim to the world. The entire evangelistic imperative of the Evangelical-Fundamentalist Movement must be seen in light of the belief in the death and resurrection of Christ.[26]

Resurrection of Christ

Closely interrelated to the other fundamentals is the doctrine of the literal resurrection of Christ. To Fundamentalists, the so-called spiritual resurrection of Christ was a totally inadequate concept. Biblically, the Scriptures clearly indicate that Christ rose bodily from the dead and appeared in a literal body form to His disciples.[27] If the justification of Christians was sealed by the death of Christ, then their ultimate regeneration was confirmed by His resurrection. Apart from the resurrection of Christ from the dead there is no Good News to tell to the world. Where Modernism was content to proclaim the moral message of Christ as summarized in the Sermon on the Mount, Fundamentalists were committed to the Gospel (the Evangel) itself. They had a message to tell to the nations because they shared with the early Church its overwhelming conviction that Jesus Christ was alive. Through their evangelistic and missionary endeavors, Fundamentalists offer to the world no mere dead moralistic teacher of the past but a living Savior who could transform a person's life today. Thus Fundamentalist-Evangelicals view themselves as relevant to humanity's needs while superseding the philosophical trends of the contemporary world.

Second Coming of Christ

Belief in the literal, bodily return of Christ is also essential to the belief of Fundamentalism. Since Jesus promised to return, and the Scriptures indicated that He would return "in like manner as ye have seen him go," the literal return of Christ is interrelated theologically to the literal resurrection of Christ. Denying modern theology's questioning whether the historical Jesus ever lived or rose again, the Fundamentalist believes that He will definitely and literally return to bring all of history to its ultimate culmination. While this doctrine is the most debated and divergent of all the fundamentals (one may choose among premillennial, postmillennial, amillennial, pretribulational, midtribulational, posttribulational, partial rapture, and other views), nevertheless all conservatives agree that Christ is coming again to judge the world and vindicate the righteous.[28] There can be no doubt that this belief has left its marked impression on American culture in general with our national insistence that a superhero will one day intervene in human history and save the world. That person will in fact be Jesus Christ Himself!

The Fundamentalist Impulse

Doctrinally, Fundamentalism is really traditional and conservative Christian orthodoxy. It arose as a defense of minimal doctrinal essentials, apart from which Christianity ceases to be Christian. The basic beliefs of the majority of fundamentalist and evangelical Christians are essentially the same as those of the majority of religious Americans. Christianity today is virtually holding to the same beliefs that were expressed by the Fundamentalists at the time of the modernist controversy earlier in this century.

CHAPTER 4

THE BIBLE: IS IT INFALLIBLE?

An understanding of the hazards in Christian fundamentalism is unattainable without a basic knowledge of the doctrine of Biblical inerrancy.* Many fundamentalists' principal approach to the Bible is based on the assumption that this doctrine is true. This chapter will consider that assumption, by examining some of the major reasons that some people are attracted to the doctrine, while others are repelled by it. In later chapters we discuss specific examples of inconsistencies or inaccuracies in the Bible.

WHAT IS THE DOCTRINE OF BIBLICAL INERRANCY?

The doctrine of Biblical inerrancy, as it is adopted by most fundamentalists, essentially maintains that the entire Bible was dictated, word for word, directly from God to the Biblical writers, and that because it was all dictated by God it must all be true, completely free from error (inerrant). While those inerrantists may allow for flexibility in their interpretation of certain verses—viewing them sometimes as, for example, allegory, symbolism , or poetry—and while some inerrantist theologians may advance such adaptations, especially when faced with difficulties in some interpretations, they will still hold the presumption of the inerrancy of the Bible, and try never to sway from that presumption. (A discussion of some

---

*In many non-technical usages the terms 'inerrant' and 'infallible' are interchangeable, both referring to exemption from error. Although we use these terms interchangeably in this book, they also have technical usages among some religious groups. For example, among some groups the term 'infallible' refers to the absolute trustworthiness of Scripture only in its teachings and doctrines, particularly those bearing on salvation. Among some other groups, the term 'inerrancy' is applied only to the original Biblical manuscripts (autographs), which are no longer available.

of the adaptations to the doctrine of Biblical inerrancy advanced by some fundamentalist and evangelical theologians is contained in Chapter 12 of this book.)

WHAT ARE ITS ATTRACTIONS?

Fundamentalists normally do not treat the doctrine of inerrancy as simply one explanation among others for the nature of the Bible. Rather, to them, the doctrine of inerrancy is more like an unquestionable law than an explanatory theory. So treated, the doctrine leads most fundamentalists to feel confident that each Biblical verse can be easily understood and applied to life's problems. Fundamentalists view the Bible as the final authority on all matters of importance in their life, and many believe that it is reliable only if it is entirely inerrant. Their approach to the Bible directly affects their views not only on obviously religious matters but on *all* matters. The well-publicized views, for example, of many fundamentalists on such topics as abortion, pornography, the family, humanism, school prayer, censorship, homosexuality, church-state relations, Communism, and national defense will not be discussed in this book, but all such views are, in their eyes, dictated in large part by their approach to the Bible. Fundamentalists, therefore, rest both their faith in God and their understandings about the world squarely upon their view of the Bible as an inerrant work.

It is, then, the apparent simplicity of Biblical inerrancy that is appealing to many fundamentalists, and that simplicity is basic to their approach not only to the Bible but also to the world around them. To many people, the doctrine of Biblical inerrancy and the fundamentalist system of thought in which it is embedded are enormously attractive. Intellectual systems generally, with their consequent orderliness, are often attractive because they help people to generalize about their experiences and the world. Indeed, thinking and talking about what one has not experienced on the basis of what one has experienced is indispensable to any abstract thinking, including scientific thinking. Scientists appeal to various canons of reasoning to predict the future on the basis of the past. For example, they talk about 'all zebras' on the basis of such zebras as have been studied.

Systems of thought that generalize about the world, then, can simplify, or at least seem to simplify, an otherwise chaotic world. The doctrine of Biblical inerrancy, however, does not exist by itself within that system. Fundamentalist teachings and fundamentalist environments, which, as discussed in the two previous chapters, often tend to discourage or minimize the importance of careful study of various Biblical interpretations, are also part of the fundamentalists' approach. Viewing the Bible as totally free from error *and* keeping any doubts about that doctrine out of mind, is an attractive approach for many people.

A system of thought that denounces all alternative ways of thinking is often enormously attractive, especially in times of widespread moral and religious uncertainty. It offers an anchor in the whirlpool of cultural change. By requiring uncritical acceptance of black-and-white definitions, such systems of thought can appeal to millions of people, who find ambiguity and ambivalence disturbing. People rarely want to admit to others or even to themselves that there are many different ways of looking at and evaluating their most treasured beliefs. It is far easier for people to believe that their way of thinking is *the* way, and that all other understandings must be misunderstandings.

WHAT ARE ITS DRAWBACKS?

It must be pointed out that, even though fundamentalists' approach to the Bible typically imparts oversimple answers, the people who adopt the doctrine of inerrancy are *not* stupid. In fact, the doctrine often functions within a system of thought that possesses a considerable degree of logical coherence, though it is a logic that is often opposed to modern scientific methods (a fact that many fundamentalists readily acknowledge). Nonetheless, there are serious moral and intellectual problems with the doctrine of inerrancy. It is false to the Bible, to science, and perhaps even to the idea of a good Creator.

The most serious problem with the fundamentalists' approach to the Bible may not necessarily be that it affirms the inerrancy of the Bible. Rather, the most serious problem with it is perhaps that it is preoccupied with the issue of inerrancy in the first place. Such a preoccupation with the issue of inerrancy reflects an understanding that probably would not be found even in most atheists. 'Either the Bible is without error or it is morally and religiously worthless.' By thinking in those polarities, many fundamentalists subscribe to a system of thought that often distorts Scripture and contradicts science.

The Bible, in fact, nowhere directly states that all of it is inerrant. Even if there is some verse that remotely suggests that idea, it is just that: a remote suggestion. The point is that the Bible is certainly not preoccupied with its inerrancy—it does not even appear to mention it. It seems, indeed, that God would most likely prefer that people use their critical minds to study His words rather than that people risk misunderstanding those words by simply assuming something to be true that might not be true.

POTENTIAL INTELLECTUAL DIFFICULTIES WITH BIBLICAL INERRANCY

The intellectual difficulties associated with the doctrine of Biblical inerrancy lie not in its adherents' generalizations *per se* but rather in the unwillingness of its adherents to abandon certain generalizations in the face of contrary evidence. While reasonable generalizations can often make confusing things easier to understand, some generalizations oversimplify and distort the world to make it mesh with oversimple expectations. Many components of racial prejudice, for example, arise from uncritical acceptance of stereotypical overgeneralizations. Indeed, by overgeneralizing and not questioning assumptions and definitions, entire systems of thought can inadequately describe the world and fail to do justice to its complexity. Perhaps the most tragic example of oversimplified thought is Naziism, which relied on uncritical definitions of Jews and the uncritical acceptance of the idea of the Germans' being a chosen people.

In some ways, the doctrine of Biblical inerrancy forces its adherents needlessly to contradict science. Note that while the claims of many archaeologists, historians, and Biblical scholars often trouble fundamentalists, many other people do not feel that their faith is threatened by such claims, or that they must defend their faith in the face of those claims. Many fundamentalists, however, feel impelled to attack the claim, for example, that the Israelites under Joshua most likely did not conquer the city of Ai (contrary to Joshua 7:1–8:29), which archaeological evidence suggests was not occupied during Joshua's lifetime. They feel that their faith is directly threatened also when, for example, scientific data reveal that the Philistines did not enter Canaan until about 1150 B.C., about five hundred years later than the period usually associated with Abraham, whom the Bible claims spent much time in the "land of the Philistines" (Genesis 21:34). Finally, when Biblical scholars and ethicists point out, for example, Biblical expressions of racial prejudice, as in the anti-Canaanite sentiment found in Genesis 9:18–27, many fundamentalists must defend those sentiments as inerrantly expressing God's will and thus proper.

Unlike fundamentalists, many of whom have historically been opposed to the findings of science, many other religious people can appreciate that the Bible reflects, for example, a pre-scientific view of astronomy, geology, and nature generally. Quite understandably, the Biblical writers, like most people of their day, described the world largely as it appeared to their senses, and their speculation, judged by current standards, was for the most part scientifically unsophisticated. The entire Bible adopts a cosmology that most ancient people, like most medieval people, used to describe the world. (For a discussion of this subject, see Chapter 5.) Most non-fundamentalists do not feel that their faith in God or their ability to use the Bible is at all hampered by acknowledging the pre-scientific background of the Bible.

Yet most believers in Biblical inerrancy feel impelled to view the entire Bible as scientifically accurate, even those parts that may not be consistent with present scientific knowledge.

MORAL DIFFICULTIES WITH BIBLICAL INERRANCY

One reason some religious people have criticized the fundamentalists' approach to the Bible is that they believe that it insults man and is unworthy of God. The primary importance of the Bible lies not in the presence or absence of scientific and historical errors, [but in its capacity to be a source for moral and spiritual growth.]

Conflicting moral views, however, are advanced in different parts of the Bible, and they cannot be fully resolved with the assumption of inerrancy. In some parts, for example, God is pictured as partial and vengeful (see Chapter 6 for a number of examples), and sometimes, therefore, the view that all people are equally important and equally worthy of moral consideration is foreign to parts of the Bible. Those examples of limited moral concern, however, contrast sharply with other parts of the Bible, covering, for instance, the times of the later prophets and Jesus, who taught universal love and universal moral concern. The moral concern of the Hebrews was a hard-won insight whose progress the Bible demonstrates magnificently. Yet applying the doctrine of Biblical inerrancy, people are required somehow to accept such divergent moral viewpoints. The result usually distorts the moral value of the Bible and ultimately the view of God's morality.

ANOTHER APPROACH TO THE BIBLE

The Bible nowhere describes Biblical authors as being made temporarily perfect or infallible for the purpose of writing the Bible while at all other times being, like most people, imperfect and fallible. Even if such exceptional occurrences did take place, it would be puzzling to many people. For why would God take control of the Biblical writers, temporarily making them infallible, displacing their humanity, and using them as mechanical mouthpieces, dictating to them exactly what they had to say and write, when He surely must have a number of other methods of communicating that would be more sensitive to the human intelligence? God has, indeed, provided mankind with an excellent source of inspiration and guidance in the form of the Bible, but it is of maximum usefulness only when people use their minds, which He created, to decide what is probably true, and what is probably not true.

That some fundamentalist teachings and environments often tend to discourage careful study of various interpretations further compounds potential intellectual difficulties. If people who adopt the doctrine of inerrancy are inquisitive about other points of view, then they can at least be cautious about those verses, laws, principles, beliefs, or interpretations that may contradict their own reasonable, and morally acceptable, judgments. They can try to avoid those ideas, even if they still do not want to stop viewing the Bible as theoretically inerrant. Yet because of the opposition to thinking about other viewpoints, many people do not exercise such critical thought.

At least one Biblical scholar who does not adopt the doctrine of Biblical inerrancy makes the following observations. His words certainly do not express the *only* possible viewpoint, but they do serve to illustrate another approach that many people may find helpful:

> Is one to take historical error, limited scientific knowledge, and human prejudice as indication of divine dictation or as a clear sign that man himself is the author and interpreter of the materials? Obviously, the latter is preferable, for it is . . . in this choice that one avoids a problematic view of God and a demeaning portrait of man. . . . [I]n this perspective . . . man become[s] a meaningful, self-determining agent rather than a puppet. And if the Biblical record is clear on any point, it is that man was created to be a free agent capable of choice and determination.
>
> Thus much depends on our basic attitude toward the Bible, how we would describe the volume as a literary product. *The Bible is man's understanding of his encounter with God.* In such a view the integrity of both God and man are preserved [and] the record [is] consistent with its evolution, transmission, and ultimate canonical status. (Frank Eakin, Jr., *Religion in Western Culture*, pp. 24–25)

THE ULTIMATE CONCERN

People may disagree with that view, but one thing must be said: In their search for the messages of God or truth in anything, people must not limit themselves to one, fixed approach that supposedly reaches '*the* truth', while it denies the possibility of many other avenues to, and forms of, truth. People may have found truth in the Bible by studying it as history, as literature, as myth, as symbol, or even as science or literal truth; but whichever path they have taken, they should try to be as honest, sensitive, and thoughtful as they can.

Most fundamentalists are pursuers of truth. They show moral courage. They want to preserve the family unit. They want their children to be loving people who do not harm themselves and who always respect others. They want to keep alive the freshness of the Christian message, especially to love thy neighbor, to resist temptations to be unkind, and to turn the other cheek when harmed by others. They give to charity, and encourage others to do likewise. They worry about sexual promiscuity, hunger, sickness, drug abuse, and other problems. They are devoted to their beliefs, and they are prepared to state their views and to hold fast to them, even when these may be unpopular.

Yet with all of these excellent qualities acknowledged, the doctrine of Biblical inerrancy is nonetheless, in effect, an intellectually incomplete approach to truth. Fundamentalists may have discovered truth through the good things that they do and the kind thoughts that they carry in their hearts, but it is questionable whether their approach to the Bible is a completely fair, sensitive, and honest approach to God or truth. Since most fundamentalists believe that any Biblical 'error' is incompatible with Divine perfection, they cannot allow anything to count as a Biblical inconsistency or implausibility. Such an unquestioned presupposition, however, is not most likely a product of impartial research.

CONCLUSION

The doctrine of Biblical inerrancy is fraught with intellectual difficulties. Further, fundamentalists who choose to hold the doctrine of inerrancy face the serious hazard of being unable to recognize and acknowledge whatever inconsistencies may exist in the Bible.

Yet the Bible has a rich diversity of understanding, ranging from the cosmology of the universe to the morality of its times and cultures, and it has, therefore, many sources of potential inconsistencies. In the face of numerous opportunities for the Bible to contain inconsistencies, people who view the Bible with such ideas as 'perfection', 'inerrancy', or 'infallibility' face constant challenges to their faith. The inability to recognize and acknowledge inconsistencies can easily lead to a decreased ability to make the wisest use of the Bible.

The greatest danger is that people who hold the doctrine of Biblical inerrancy may, even unintentionally, come to accept insulting conceptions of the world, mankind, and God. The next few chapters will examine in detail various aspects of the Bible that, when viewed as 'inerrant', are often not adequately appreciated and can therefore contribute to a distorted portrait of God and the Bible.

and authority. But there is one thing which I cannot despise, and that is my excuse for writing once more to thy Blessedness. I understand that I am accused of great rashness, and that this rashness is said to be my great fault, in which, they say, I have not spared even thy person.

For my part, I will openly confess that I know I have only spoken good and honorable things of thee whenever I have made mention of thy name. . . . I have indeed sharply inveighed against ungodly teachings in general, and I have not been slow to bite my adversaries, not because of their immorality, but because of their ungodliness. And of this I repent so little that I have determined to persevere in that fervent zeal, and to despise the judgment of men, following the example of Christ, Who in His zeal called His adversaries a generation of vipers, blind, hypocrites, children of the devil. . . . Nowadays, it is true, our ears are made so delicate by the mad crowds of flatterers that as soon as we meet with a disapproving voice we cry out that we are bitten, and when we cannot ward off the truth with any other pretext we put it to flight by ascribing it to a fierce temper, impatience and shamelessness. What is the good of salt if it does not bite? Or of the edge of the sword if it does not kill? Cursed be he that doeth the work of the Lord deceitfully. . . .

.   .   .   .   .

But thy See, which is called the Roman Curia, and of which neither thou nor any man can deny that it is more corrupt than any Babylon or Sodom ever was, and which is, as far as I can see, characterized by a totally depraved, hopeless and notorious wickedness —that See I have truly despised, and I have been incensed to think that in thy name and under the guise of the Roman Church the people of Christ are mocked. And so I have resisted and will resist that See, as long as the spirit of faith shall live in me. Not that I shall strive after the impossible in that most disordered Babylon, where the rage of so many sycophants is turned against me; but I acknowledge myself a debtor to my brethren, whom it is my duty to warn, that fewer of

6. *Luther's Treatise on Christian Liberty, 1520*

Works of Martin Luther, II, trans. W. A. Lambert (Philadelphia: Muhlenberg Press, 1943).

LUTHER'S LETTER TO POPE LEO X

To Leo the Tenth, Pope at Rome: Martin Luther wishes thee salvation in Christ Jesus our Lord. Amen.

In the midst of the monsters of this age with whom I am now for the third year waging war, I am compelled at times to look up also to thee, Leo, most blessed Father, and to think of thee; nay, since thou art now and again regarded as the sole cause of my warfare, I cannot but think of thee always. . . . It is true, I have made bold almost to despise and to triumph over those who have tried to frighten me with the majesty of thy name

22

them may be destroyed by the plagues of Rome, or at least that their destruction may be less cruel.

For, as thou well knowest, these many years there has flowed forth from Rome, like a flood covering the world, nothing but a laying waste of men's bodies and souls and possessions, and the worst possible examples of the worst possible things. For all this is clearer than the day to all men, and the Roman Church, once the most holy of all, has become the most licentious den of thieves, the most shameless of all brothels, the kingdom of sin, death and hell; so that even Antichrist himself, should he come, could think of nothing to add to its wickedness.

Meanwhile thou, Leo, sittest as a lamb in the midst of wolves, like Daniel in the midst of lions, and, with Ezekiel, thou dwellest among scorpions. What canst thou do singlehanded, against these monsters? Join to thyself three or four thoroughly learned and thoroughly good cardinals: what are even these among so many? You would all be poisoned before you could undertake to make a single decree to help matters. . . . The Roman Curia has not deserved to have thee or men like thee, but rather Satan himself; and in truth it is he more than thou who rules in that Babylon.

.   .   .   .   .   .

To go yet farther, I never intended to inveigh against the Roman Curia, or to raise any controversy concerning it. For when I saw that all efforts to save it were hopeless, I despised it and gave it a bill of divorcement and said to it, "He that is filthy, let him be filthy still, and he that is unclean, let him be unclean still." Then I gave myself to the quiet and peaceful study of holy Scripture, that I might thus be of benefit to my brethren about me. When I had made some progress in these studies, Satan opened his eyes and filled his servant John Eck, a notable enemy of Christ, with an insatiable lust for glory, and thereby stirred him up to drag me at unawares into a disputation, laying hold on me by one little word about the primacy of the Roman Church which I had inci-

dentally let fall. Then that boasting braggart, frothing and gnashing his teeth, declared that he would venture all for the glory of God and the honor of the holy Apostolic See, and, puffed up with the hope of misusing thy power, he looked forward with perfect confidence to a victory over me. He sought not so much to establish the primacy of Peter as his own leadership among the theologians of our time; and to that end he thought it no small help if he should triumph over Luther. When that debate ended unhappily for the sophist, an incredible madness overcame the man: for he feels that he alone must bear the blame of all that I have brought forth to the shame of Rome.

But permit me, I pray thee, most excellent Leo, this once to plead my cause and to make charges against thy real enemies. Thou knowest, I believe, what dealings thy legate, Cardinal of St. Sixtus [Cajetan], an unwise and unfortunate, or rather, unfaithful man, had with me. When, because of reverence for thy name, I at that time promised to keep silent and to end the controversy, if my opponents were ordered to do the same. But as he was a man who sought glory, and was not content with that agreement, he began to justify my opponents, to give them full freedom and to order me to recant, a thing not included in his instructions. . . .

Next came Carl Miltitz. . . . Again I yielded to your name, I was prepared to keep silent, and even accepted as arbiter either the archbishop of Treves or the bishop of Naumburg. So matters were arranged. But while this plan was being followed with good prospects of success, lo, that other and greater enemy of thine, Eck, broke in with the Leipzig Disputation [June 27-July 15, 1519] which he had undertaken against Dr. Carlstadt. When a new question concerning the primacy of the pope was raised, he suddenly turned his weapons against me and quite overthrew that counsel of peace. Meanwhile Carl Miltitz waited: a disputation was held, judges were selected; but here also no decision was reached, and no wonder: through the lies, the tricks, the wiles of Eck everything was stirred up, aggravated and confounded worse than ever, so that whatever decision might have been reached, a greater conflagration would have resulted. For he sought glory, not the truth. . . .

Since we gained nothing by this disputation except that we brought great confusion to the cause of Rome, Carl Miltitz made a third attempt; he came to the fathers of the Augustinian Order assembled in their chapter, and asked counsel in settling the controversy which had now grown most confused and dangerous. Since, by the favor of God, they had no hope of being able to proceed against me with violence, some of the most famous of their number were sent to me, and asked me at least to show honor to the person of thy Blessedness, and in a humble letter to plead as my excuse thy innocence and mine; they said that the affair was not yet in the most desperate state if of his innate goodness Leo the Tenth would take a hand in it. . . .

So I come, most blessed Father, and, prostrate before thee, I pray, if it be possible do thou interpose and hold in check those flatterers, who are the enemies of peace while they pretend to keep peace. But that I will recant, most blessed Father, let no one imagine, unless he prefer to involve the whole question in greater turmoil. Furthermore, I will accept no rules for the interpretation of the Word of God, since the Word of God, which teaches the liberty of all things else, dare not be bound. Grant me these two points, and there is nothing that I could not or would not most gladly do or endure. I hate disputations; I will draw out no one; but then I do not wish others to draw me out; if they do, as Christ is my Teacher, I will not be speechless. For, when once this controversy has been cited before thee and settled, thy Blessedness will be able with a small and easy word to silence both parties and command them to keep the peace, and that is what I have always wished to hear.

Do not listen, therefore, my dear Leo, to those sirens who make thee out to be no mere man but a demigod, so that thou mayest command and require what thou wilt.

. . . . . .

Finally, that I may not approach thee empty-handed, blessed Father, I bring with me this little treatise published under thy name as an omen of peace and of good hope. From this book thou mayest judge with what studies I would prefer to be more profitably engaged, as I could be if your godless flatterers would permit me, and had hitherto permitted me. May the Lord Jesus preserve thee forever. Amen. (*Wittenberg, September 6, 1520.*)

A TREATISE ON CHRISTIAN LIBERTY

A Christian man is a perfectly free lord of all, subject to none.

A Christian man is a perfectly dutiful servant of all, subject to all.

Although these two theses seem to contradict each other, yet, if they should be found to fit together they would serve our purpose beautifully. For they are both Paul's own, who says, in I Cor. 9, "Whereas I was free, I made myself the servant of all," and, Rom. 13, "Owe no man anything, but to love one another." Now love by its very nature is ready to serve and to be subject to him who is loved. So, Christ, although Lord of all, was made of a woman, made under the law, and hence was at the same time free and a servant, at the same time in the form of God and in the form of a servant.

Let us start, however, with something more obvious. Man has a twofold nature, a spiritual and a bodily, [and these two] contradict each other, since the flesh lusteth against the spirit and the spirit against the flesh (Gal. 5).

First, let us contemplate the inward man, to see how a righteous, free and truly Christian man, that is, a new, spiritual, inward man, comes into being. It is evident that no external thing, whatsoever it be, has any influence whatever in producing Christian righteousness or liberty, nor in producing unrighteousness or bondage. A simple argument will furnish the proof. What can it profit the soul if the body fare well, be free and active, eat, drink and do as it pleases? For in these things even the most godless slaves of all the vices fare well. On the other hand, how will ill health or imprisonment or hunger or thirst or any other external misfortune

24

hurt the soul? With these things even the most godly men are afflicted, and those who because of a clear conscience are most free. None of these things touch either the liberty or the bondage of the soul. The soul receives no benefit if the body is adorned with the sacred robes of the priesthood, or dwells in sacred places, or is occupied with sacred duties, or prays, fasts, abstains from certain kinds of food or does any work whatsoever that can be done by the body and in the body.... On the other hand, it will not hurt the soul if the body is clothed in secular dress, dwells in unconsecrated places, eats and drinks as others do, does not pray aloud, and neglects to do all the things mentioned above, which hypocrites can do.

One thing and one only is necessary for Christian life, righteousness and liberty. That one thing is the most holy Word of God, the Gospel of Christ.... You ask, "What then is this Word of God, and how shall it be used, since there are so many words of God?" I answer, The Apostle explains that in Romans 1. The Word is the Gospel of God concerning his Son, Who was made flesh, suffered, rose from the dead, and was glorified through the Spirit Who sanctifies. For to preach Christ means to feed the soul, to make it righteous, to set it free and to save it, if it believe the preaching. For faith alone is the saving and efficacious use of the Word of God, Romans 10, "If thou confess with thy mouth that Jesus is Lord, and believe with thy heart that God hath raised Him up from the dead, thou shalt be saved"; and again, "The end of the law is Christ, unto righteousness to every one that believeth"; and, Romans 1, "The just shall live by his faith." The Word of God cannot be received and cherished by any works whatever, but only by faith. Hence it is clear that, as the soul needs only the Word for its life and righteousness, so it is justified by faith alone and not by any works; for if it could be justified by anything else, it would not need the Word, and therefore it would not need faith. But this faith cannot at all exist in connection with works, that is to say, if you at the same time claim to be justified by works, whatever their character; for that would be to halt between two sides, to wor-

ship Baal and to kiss the hand, which, as Job says, is a very great iniquity.... When you have learned this, you will know that you need Christ, Who suffered and rose again for you, that, believing in Him, you may through this faith become a new man, in that all your sins are forgiven, and you are justified by the merits of another, namely, of Christ alone.

Since, therefore, this faith can rule only in the inward man, as Romans 10 says, "With the heart we believe unto righteousness"; and since faith alone justifies, it is clear that the inward man cannot be justified, made free and be saved by any outward work or dealing whatsoever, and that works, whatever their character, have nothing to do with this inward man.... Wherefore it ought to be the first concern of every Christian to lay aside all trust in works, and more and more to strengthen faith alone, and through faith to grow in the knowledge, not of works, but of Christ Jesus.

Should you ask, how it comes that faith alone justifies and without works offers us such a treasury of great benefits, when so many works, ceremonies and laws are prescribed in the Scriptures, I answer: First of all, remember what has been said: faith alone, without works, justifies, makes free and saves, as we shall later make still more clear. Here we must point out that all the Scriptures of God are divided into two parts —commands and promises. The commands indeed teach things that are good, but the things taught are not done as soon as taught; for the commands show us what we ought to do, but do not give us the power to do it; they are intended to teach a man to know himself, that through them he may recognize his inability to do good and may despair of his powers. That is why they are called and are the Old Testament....

But when a man through the commands has learned to know his weakness, and has become troubled as to how he may satisfy the law, since the law must be fulfilled so that not a jot or tittle shall perish, otherwise man will be condemned without hope; then, being truly humbled and reduced to nothing in his own eyes, he finds in himself no means of justification and salvation. Here the second part of the Scriptures stands ready—the promises of God, which declare the glory of God and say, "If you wish to fulfil the law, and not to covet, as the law demands. come, believe in Christ, in Whom grace, righteousness, peace, liberty and all things are promised you; if you believe you shall have all, if you believe not you shall lack all." For what is impossible for you in all the works of the law, many as they are, but all useless, you will accomplish in a short and easy way through faith. For God our Father has made all things depend on faith, so that whoever has faith, shall have all, and whoever has it not, shall have nothing. "For He has concluded all under unbelief, that He might have mercy on all," Romans 11. Thus the promises of God give what the commands of God ask, and fulfil what the law prescribes, that all things may be of God alone, both the commands and the fulfilling of the commands. He alone commands, He also alone fulfils. Therefore the promises of God belong to the New Testament, nay, they are the New Testament....

No work can cling to the Word of God nor be in the soul; in the soul faith alone and the Word have sway. As the Word is, so it makes the soul, as heated iron glows like fire because of the union of fire with it. It is clear then that a Christian man has in his faith all that he needs, and needs no works to justify him. And if he has no need of works, neither does he need the law; and if he has no need of the law, surely he is free from the law, and it is true, "The law is not made for a righteous man." And this is that Christian liberty, even our faith, which does not indeed cause us to live in idleness or in wickedness, but makes the law and works unnecessary for any man's righteousness and salvation.

This is the first power of faith. Let us now examine the second also. For it is a further function of faith, that whom it trusts it also honors with the most reverent and high regard, since it considers him truthful and trustworthy.... So when the soul firmly trusts God's promises, it regards Him as truthful and righteous, than which nothing more excellent can be ascribed to God. This is the very highest worship of God.... Then the soul consents to all His will, then it hallows His name and suffers itself to be dealt with according to God's good pleasure, because, clinging to God's promises, it does not doubt that He, Who is true, just and wise, will do, dispose and provide all things well. And is not such a soul, by this faith, in all things most obedient to God? ...

The third incomparable benefit of faith is this, that it unites the soul with Christ as a bride is united with her bridegroom. And by this mystery, as the Apostle teaches, Christ and the soul become one flesh....

Who can fully appreciate what this royal marriage means? Who can understand the riches of the glory of this grace? Here this rich and godly Bridegroom Christ marries this poor, wicked harlot, redeems her from all her evil and adorns her with all His good. It is now impossible that her sins should destroy her, since they are laid upon Christ and swallowed up in Him, and she has that righteousness in Christ her husband of which she may boast as of her own, and which she can confidently set against all her sins in the face of death and hell....

Just as Christ by his birthright obtained these two prerogatives (priesthood and kingship), so He imparts them to and shares them with every one who believes on Him according to the law of the aforesaid marriage, by which the wife owns whatever belongs to the husband. Hence we are all priests and kings in Christ, as many as believe on Christ, as I Pet. 2 says, "Ye are a chosen generation, a peculiar people, a royal priesthood and priestly kingdom, that ye should show forth the virtues of Him Who hath called you out of darkness into His marvelous light...."

Not only are we the freest of kings, we are also priests forever, which is far more excellent than being kings, because as priests we are worthy to appear before God to pray for others and to teach one another the things of God. For these are the functions of priests, and cannot be granted to any unbeliever. Thus Christ has obtained for us, if we believe on Him, that we are not only His brethren, co-heirs and fellow-kings with Him, but also fellow-priests with Him, who may boldly come into the presence of God in the spirit of faith....

26

A Christian man is free from all things and over all things, so that he needs no works to make him righteous and to save him, since faith alone confers all these abundantly. But should he grow so foolish as to presume to become righteous by means of some good work, he would on the instant lose faith and all its benefits: a foolishness aptly illustrated in the fable of the dog who runs along a stream with a piece of meat in his mouth, and, deceived by the reflection of the meat in the water, opens his mouth to snap at it, and so loses both the meat and the reflection.

You will ask, "If all who are in the Church are priests, how do those whom we now call priests differ from laymen?" I answer: "Injustice is done those words, 'priest,' 'cleric,' 'spiritual,' 'ecclesiastic,' when they are transferred from all other Christians to those few who are now by a mischievous usage called 'ecclesiastics.' For Holy Scripture makes no distinction between them, except that it gives the name 'ministers,' 'servants,' 'stewards,' to those who are now proudly called popes, bishops, and lords and who should by the ministry of the Word serve others and teach them the faith of Christ and the liberty of believers. For although we are all equally priests, yet we cannot all publicly minister and teach, nor ought we if we could."

But that stewardship has now been developed into so great a pomp of power and so terrible a tyranny, that no heathen empire or earthly power can be compared with it, just as if laymen were not also Christians. Through this perversion the knowledge of Christian grace, faith, liberty and of Christ Himself has altogether perished, and its place has been taken by an unbearable bondage of human words and laws. . . .

Now let us turn to the second part, to the outward man. Here we shall answer all those who, misled by the word "faith" and by all that has been said, now say: "If faith does all things and is alone sufficient unto righteousness, why then are good works commanded? We will take our ease and do no works, and be content with faith." I answer, Not so, ye wicked men, not so. That would indeed be proper, if we were wholly inward and perfectly spiritual men; but such we shall be only at the last day, the day of the resur-

rection of the dead. As long as we live in the flesh we only begin and make some progress in that which shall be perfected in the future life. . . .

Although, as I have said, a man is abundantly justified by faith inwardly, in his spirit, and so has all that he ought to have, except in so far as this faith and riches must grow from day to day even unto the future life: yet he remains in this mortal life on earth, and in this life he must needs govern his own body and have dealings with men. Here the works begin; here a man cannot take his ease; here he must, indeed, take care to discipline his body by fastings, watchings, labors and other reasonable discipline, and to make it subject to the spirit so that it will obey and conform to the inward man and to faith, and not revolt against faith and hinder the inward man, as it is the body's nature to do if it be not held in check. For the inward man, who by faith is created in the likeness of God, is both joyful and happy because of Christ in Whom so many benefits are conferred upon him, and therefore it is his one occupation to serve God joyfully and for naught, in love that is not constrained.

In doing these works, however, we must not think that a man is justified before God by them: for that erroneous opinion faith, which alone is righteousness before God, cannot endure; but we must think that these works reduce the body to subjection and purify it of its evil lusts, and our whole purpose is to be directed only toward the driving out of lusts. For since by faith the soul is cleansed and made a lover of God, it desires that all things, and especially its own body, shall be as pure as itself, so that all things may join with it in loving and praising God. Hence a man cannot be idle, because the need of his body drives him and he is compelled to do many good works to reduce it to subjection. Nevertheless the works themselves do not justify him before God, but he does the works out of spontaneous love in obedience to God, and considers nothing except the approval of God, Whom he would in all things most scrupulously obey.

In this way every one will easily be able to learn for himself the limit and discretion, as they say, of his bodily castigations: for he will fast, watch and labor as much as he finds sufficient to repress the lasciviousness and lust of his body. But they who presume to be justified by works do not regard the mortifying of the lusts, but only the works themselves, and think that if only they have done as many and as great works as are possible, they have done well, and have become righteousness; at times they even addle their brains and destroy, or at least render useless, their natural strength with their works. This is the height of folly, and utter ignorance of Christian life and faith, that a man should seek to be justified and saved by works and without faith.

.   .   .   .   .   .

But none of these things does a man need for his righteousness and salvation. Therefore, in all his works he should be guided by this thought and look to this one thing alone, that he may serve and benefit others in all that he does, having regard to nothing except the need and the advantage of his neighbor. Thus, the Apostle commands us to work with our hands that we may give to him who is in need, although he might have said that we should work to support ourselves. And this is what makes it a Christian work to care for the body, that through its health and comfort we may be able to work, to acquire and to lay by funds with which to aid those who are in need, that in this way the strong member may serve the weaker, and we may be sons of God, each caring for and working for the other, bearing one another's burdens, and so fulfilling the law of Christ. Lo, this is a truly Christian life, here faith is truly effectual through love; that is, it issues in works of the freest service cheerfully and lovingly done, with which a man willingly serves another without hope of reward, and for himself is satisfied with the fullness and wealth of his faith....

Although the Christian is thus free from all works, he ought in this liberty to empty himself, to take upon himself the form of a servant, to be made in the likeness of men, to be found in fashion as a man, and to serve, help and in every way deal with his neighbor as he sees that God through Christ has dealt and still deals with himself. And this he should do freely, having regard to nothing except the divine approval. He ought to think: "Though I am an unworthy and condemned man, my God has given me in Christ all the riches of righteousness and salvation without any merit on my part, out of pure, free mercy, so that henceforth I need nothing whatever except faith which believes that this is true. Why should I not therefore freely, joyfully, with all my heart, and with an eager will, do all things which I know are pleasing and acceptable to such a Father, Who has overwhelmed with His inestimable riches? I will therefore give myself as a Christ to my neighbor, just as Christ offered Himself to me; I will do nothing in this life except what I see is necessary, profitable and salutary to my neighbor, since through faith I have an abundance of all good things in Christ."

Lo, thus from faith flow forth love and joy in the Lord, and from love a joyful, willing and free mind that serves one's neighbor willingly and takes no account of gratitude or ingratitude, of praise or blame, of gain or loss. For a man does not serve that he may put men under obligations, he does not distinguish between friends and enemies, nor does he anticipate their thankfulness or unthankfulness; but most freely and most willingly he spends himself and all that he has, whether he waste all on the thankless or whether he gain a reward. For as his Father does, distributing all things to all men richly and freely, causing His sun to rise upon the good and upon the evil, so also the son does all things and suffers all things with that freely bestowing joy which is his delight when through Christ he sees it in God, the dispenser of such great benefits.

Therefore, if we recognize the great and precious things which are given us, as Paul says, there will be shed abroad in our hearts by the Holy Ghost the love which makes us free, joyful, almighty workers and conquerors over all tribulations, servants of our neighbors and yet lords of all. But for those who do not recognize the gifts bestowed upon them through Christ, Christ has been born in vain: they go their way with their works, and shall never come to taste or to feel those

28

II
The Christian View
of Other Faiths

The traditional Christian attitude to other faiths was formed in a period of substantial ignorance of the wider religious life of mankind, and it has recently been thrown into a ferment of rethinking by greater and more widespread knowledge.

We can distinguish three phases so far in the development of the Christian attitude to the other world religions.

1. The first phase—the phase of total rejection—was expressed in the dogma that non-Christians, as such, are consigned to hell. As the expression of an attitude to other human beings the dogma is as arrogant as it is cruel; and it is a sobering thought that such a dogma was at one time almost universally accepted among Christians. In the medieval formulations, Christians were of course equated with those acknowledging the supremacy of the Roman pope. Thus we read in a papal pronouncement of Boniface VIII in 1302: "We are required by faith to believe and hold that there is one holy, catholic and apostolic Church; we firmly believe it and unreservedly profess it; outside it there is neither salvation nor remission of sins. . . . Further, we declare, say, define and proclaim that to submit to the Roman Pontiff is, for every human creature, an utter necessity of salvation." (Denzinger, *Enchiridion Symbolorum Definitionum et Declarationum de Rebus Fidei et Morum*, 29th

ed., No. 468f.; Freiburg, 1952.) Again, the Council of Florence (1438–45) affirmed that "no one remaining outside the Catholic Church, not just pagans, but also Jews or heretics or schismatics, can become partakers of eternal life; but they will go to the 'everlasting fire which was prepared for the devil and his angels,' unless before the end of life they are joined to the Church" (Denzinger, No. 714).

The Roman Catholic Church today has passed decisively beyond this phase, but the earlier dogma still persists within evangelical-fundamentalist Protestantism. For example, one of the messages of the Congress on World Mission at Chicago in 1960 declared: "In the years since the war, more than one billion souls have passed into eternity and more than half of these went to the torment of hell fire without even hearing of Jesus Christ, who He was, or why He died on the cross of Calvary." (*Facing the Unfinished Task: Messages Delivered at the Congress on World Mission*, Chicago, Ill., 1960, ed. by J. O. Percy, p. 9; Wm. B. Eerdmans Publishing Co., 1961.) The main difference between the medieval Catholic dogma and this is that whereas the former assumed that Christians are those owing obedience to the pope, the latter is inclined to doubt whether the pope and his followers are Christians at all!

This entirely negative attitude to other faiths is strongly correlated with ignorance of them. There was of course contact in the medieval period between Christianity and Islam; but it was a military contact, not a religious dialogue or a mutual exploration of one another's spirituality. The average Christian's distorted conceptions of Islam were matched only by the average Muslim's distorted conceptions of Christianity. Today, however, the extreme evangelical Protestant who believes that all Muslims go to hell is probably not so much ignorant (for he has some missionary contact with Islam, and an enormous literature is available about the world religions) as blinded by dark dogmatic spectacles through which he can see no good in religious devotion outside his own group.

But the basic weakness in this attitude of rejection lies in the doctrine of God which it presupposes. If all human beings must, in order to attain the eternal happiness for which they have been created, accept Jesus Christ as their Lord and Savior before they die, then the great majority of humanity is doomed to eternal frustration and misery. For the vast majority of those who have ever been born lived either before Christ or outside the range of his historical influence and could not respond to him with saving faith. To say that such an appalling situation is divinely ordained is to deny the Christian understanding of God as gracious and holy love, and of Christ as the divine love incarnate. Thus the attitude of total rejection, expressed in the dogma that outside Christianity there is no salvation, implies a conception of God radically questionable from the standpoint of Christian faith.

2. The second phase—which I shall call the phase of the early epicycles—arose out of a growing awareness among Catholic thinkers of the reality of religious faith, first among Protestant Christians and then among devout men of the great non-Christian religions. The response was to retain the words of the established dogma but to add a rider reversing its practical effect. The dogma thus stands that only Catholics can be saved (*Extra ecclesiam nulla salus*), but it is declared of various people who, empirically, are not Catholics that they may nevertheless, metaphysically, be Catholics without knowing it! There is an analogy here with the dogma of transubstantiation: to human observation the bread and wine remain bread and wine, but their metaphysical substance is said to become that of the body and blood of Christ. Likewise, devout Protestants, Jews, Muslims, Hindus, etc., may remain Hindus, Muslims, Jews, and Protestants, and themselves believe that this is what they are, but they

may nevertheless—metaphysically—be redeemed members of the mystical body of Christ. They may belong to the invisible, as distinguished from the visible, church; or they may be invincibly, and therefore nonculpably, ignorant of the truth of the Catholic faith, and so disposed that they *would* accept it if they genuinely encountered it; or they may have implicit instead of explicit faith; or they may have been baptized by desire, namely their sincere desire for the truth even though they do not yet know what the truth is; or, in a Protestant variant, they may belong to the latent as distinguished from the manifest church.

These are all variations on a common theme. We see the theme being deployed in, for example, the allocution of Pope Pius IX in 1854: "It must, of course, be held as a matter of faith that outside the apostolic Roman Church no one can be saved, that the Church is the only ark of salvation, and that whoever does not enter it will perish in the flood. On the other hand, it must likewise be held as certain that those who are affected by ignorance of the true religion, if it is invincible ignorance, are not subject to any guilt in this matter before the eyes of the Lord" (Denzinger, No. 1647). Or again, in the important 1949 letter from the Holy Office in Rome to the Archbishop of Boston: "To gain eternal salvation it is not always required that a person be incorporated in fact as a member of the Church, but it is required that he belong to it at least in desire and longing. It is not always necessary that this desire be explicit.... When a man is invincibly ignorant, God also accepts an implicit desire, so called because it is contained in the good disposition of soul by which a man wants his will to be conformed to God's will." (*The Church Teaches*, pp. 274f.; St. Louis and London: B. Herder Book Co., 1955.)

I call these supplementary concepts epicycles because they are strongly reminiscent of the epicycles that were added to the old Ptolemaic picture of the universe, with the earth at the center, in an attempt to accommodate increasingly accurate knowledge of the paths of the planets. The heavenly bodies were all supposed to move in concentric circles around the earth. This was at one time a plausible theory as regards the stars; but the planets' paths, as they became known, did not conform to the scheme. However, instead of abandoning the scheme the ancient astronomers added a series of smaller supplementary circles, called epicycles, revolving with their centers on the original circles. If a planet was thought of as moving on one of these smaller circles, while it was in turn moving around the great circle, the resulting path was more complex and nearer to what was actually observed; and this complication of the system made it possible to maintain the basic dogma that our earth is the hub of the universe. In theory it was possible to stick indefinitely to the faith that the earth is the center, adding epicycle upon epicycle to reconcile this theory with the facts. However, such a system became increasingly contrived and burdensome; and the time came when people's minds were ready for the new Copernican conception that it is the sun and not the earth that is at the center. Then the old Ptolemaic picture was thrown aside and was soon seen in retrospect as utterly antiquated and implausible. It may well be that much the same will apply to the Ptolemaic theology whose fixed point is the principle that outside the church, or outside Christianity, there is no salvation. When we find persons of other faiths to be devout, we add an epicycle of theory to the effect that although they are consciously adherents of another faith, nevertheless they may unconsciously or implicitly be Christians. There is no point at which such maneuvers become logically impossible; but nevertheless their intellectual cost can mount to an unacceptable level.

3. During the last few decades, and particularly since Vatican II, a third phase, which we may call that of the "later" epicycles, has been evident. Here theological ingenuity goes to its limits to hold together the two

propositions that outside Christianity there is *no* salvation, and that outside Christianity there *is* salvation! The second of these propositions acknowledges an evident fact. For if the idea of salvation is given any experiential content, in terms of, for example, human renewal, liberation, re-creation, becoming a new creature, or achieving an authentically human existence, then it is manifestly the case that such transforming experiences occur outside as well as inside Christianity. Accordingly, the first proposition has had to be reinterpreted to bring it into harmony with the second. This is achieved by tacitly converting it from a factual assertion into a stipulative definition. Instead of being the assertion that only Christians can be saved, it becomes the definitional convention that all who are saved are to be called Christians—not, however, directly, but under some oblique description. For example, Karl Rahner has contributed the notion of "anonymous" Christianity. "Christianity," he says, "does not simply confront the member of an extra-Christian religion as a mere non-Christian but as someone who can and must be regarded in this or that respect as an anonymous Christian." (*Theological Investigations*, Vol. 5, 1966, p. 131; London: Darton, Longman & Todd; New York: Seabury Press.) This seems a bold and world-ecumenical utterance; and yet, on analysis, it does not in substance go any further than the early epicycles. The anonymous Christian is the invincibly ignorant man of implicit faith, who is baptized by desire, and who therefore belongs to the invisible church. However, Hans Küng's more daring proposal looks like a genuine advance. He distinguishes between the ordinary way of salvation within the world religions and the extraordinary way within the Catholic Church. "A man is to be saved," he says, "within the religion that is made available to him in his historical situation." (In Joseph Neuner, ed., *Christian Revelation and World Religions*, p. 52; London: Burns & Oates, 1967.) Thus the world religions are, he says, "the way of salvation in universal salvation history; the general way of salvation, we can even say, for the people of the world religions: the more common, the 'ordinary' way of salvation, as against which the way of salvation in the Church appears as something very special and extraordinary" (Neuner, p. 53).

The orbit of Küng's epicycle is now so wide that it is in danger of flying off out of the Ptolemaic frame. For if "ordinary" were taken to mean "majority," and "extraordinary" to mean "minority," we should have a straightforward acknowledgment that most men are saved by God through religious traditions other than Christianity. However, Küng makes it clear that this is not his meaning. For him the ordinary way of salvation through the world religions is only an interim state until the adherents of those religions arrive at an explicit Christian faith. People of other faiths, he says, "are pre-Christian, directed towards Christ. . . . The men of the world religions are not professing Christians but, by the grace of God, they are called and marked out to be Christians" (Neuner, pp. 55–56). The non-Christian's right and duty to seek God within his own religion is only "until such time as he is confronted in an existential way with the revelation of Jesus Christ" (Neuner, p. 52). Thus it is clear that this is not a Copernican revolution in the Christian theology of religions but only another epicycle, sophisticated and charitable but still confined within the traditional Ptolemaic mold.

Another form of later epicycle, more readily available to the liberal Protestant than to the Roman Catholic or the evangelical fundamentalist, removes the traditional this-life restriction, and declares that although all men must sooner or later accept Christ as their Lord and Savior, they may still do this in the life to come, if they have not done it in the present existence. This is in some ways an attractive theory, though still not without its own difficulties. For if salvation is recognized as a present human experience, then it undoubtedly occurs outside Christianity as well as within it; and if salvation for the non-Christian is confined by our dogma to the world to come, we have a clash between dogma and fact.

It is understandable that a growing number of Christians seem to have lost confidence in all these theological epicycles and are open to the possibility of a Copernican revolution in our Christian attitude to other religions.

The Copernican revolution in astronomy consisted in a transformation of the way in which men understood the universe and their own location within it. It involved a radical shift from the dogma that the earth is the center of the revolving universe to the realization that the sun is at the center, with all the planets, including our own earth, moving around it. And the Copernican revolution in theology must involve an equally radical transformation of our conception of the universe of faiths and the place of our own religion within it. It must involve a shift from the dogma that Christianity is at the center to the thought that it is *God* who is at the center and that all the religions of mankind, including our own, serve and revolve around him.

I have already acknowledged that it is possible in principle to go on indefinitely thinking Ptolemaically. But we have to realize that a Ptolemaic type of theology is capable of being operated not only from within Christianity but equally from within any other faith—just as men on Mars or Jupiter, if there were any, could formulate their own Ptolemaic astronomy, with their own planet as the center of the system. The most striking non-Christian example of this today in the religious realm is provided by contemporary philosophical Hinduism. This holds that the ultimate reality, Brahman, is beyond all qualities, including personality, and that personal deities, such as the Yahweh of the Bible or the Krishna of the *Bhagavad-Gita*, are partial images of the Absolute created for the benefit of that majority of mankind who cannot rise above anthropomorphic thinking to the pure Absolute. Thus the various religions of the world, with their different proportions of anthropomorphism and mysticism, can be seen as so many approaches to the truth that is fully revealed in the Upanishads. Here we have a Ptolemaic system with a Vedantic instead of a Christian center. And from this point of view the Christian, the Jew, the Muslim, or other devout person can be said to be a Vedantist without knowing it. He is an "anonymous" Vedantist; he stands within the lower or "ordinary" realms of the religious life, but will rise eventually into the "extraordinary" realm of the truly enlightened; he is a Vedantist "implicitly" and by virtue of his sincere desire for the truth, even though he does not yet know what the truth really is; although in error in this life, he will be confronted by the truth in its full glory in the life to come and will then be converted to it. Thus all the epicycles of Ptolemaic Christianity can also be used to maintain a Ptolemaic Hinduism—or a Ptolemaic Buddhism, or Islam, or Judaism, and so on. The adherent of each tradition can assume that his own system of belief is the truth and that all the others are more or less true according as they approximate to it or diverge from it. Indeed this is a very natural assumption to make. And yet one only has to stand back in thought from the arena of competing systems, surveying the scene as a whole, to see something that is hidden from the Ptolemaic believer. This is the fact that the particular standpoint of a Ptolemaic theology normally depends upon where the believer happens to have been born! Having seen this, one can hardly help wondering whether it provides a sufficient basis for a conviction which involves an assessment of all other men's convictions. I myself used to hold a Ptolemaic Christian theology; but if I had been born into a devout Hindu family and had studied philosophy at, let us say, the University of Madras, I should probably have held a Ptolemaic Hindu theology instead. And if I had been born to Muslim parents, say in Egypt or Pakistan, I should probably have held a Ptolemaic Muslim theology. And so on. Having thus noted that Ptolemaic theologies tend to posit their centers on the basis of the accidents of geography, one is likely to see one's own Ptolemaic conviction in a new light. Can we be so entirely confident that to have been born in our particular part of the world carries with it the privilege of knowing the full religious truth, whereas to be born elsewhere involves the likelihood of having only partial and inferior truth?

It is not possible within the scope of such short space to go on to describe the new map of the universe of faiths which becomes visible when we make the Copernican revolution in our attitude to the religious life of mankind. Let me end by mentioning some of the questions that have to be answered by any acceptable view of the relation between Christianity and the other world faiths.

In relation to the history of religions, we have to ask how, if God has always been seeking to reveal himself to mankind, he might do this within the conditions of the world he has created. Since the early civilizations were largely separate, did they require different revelations? How would such revelations be related to the different mentalities of men in their different cultural and historical circumstances?

We have to ask: Are theologies to be regarded as divinely revealed bodies of knowledge, or as speculative human interpretations of man's religious experience? To what extent are the theologies of the different religious traditions ultimately compatible or incompatible? For example, can God be both personal and nonpersonal? Here we have to explore the possibility that the divine nature is infinite, exceeding the scope of all human concepts, and is capable of being experienced both as personal Lord and as nonpersonal ground and depth of being.

As Christians we have to do justice to our distinctive faith in the uniqueness of Christ as God the Son incarnate. Here we have to ask what sort of language this is. Does the mystery of the incarnation represent a literal or a mythological use of language? If the latter, what is the relation of the idea of incarnation to other religious mythologies?

And what are the implications for Christian missions of the Copernican revolution in theology? Should mission be "sideways," into cultures dominated by other great world faiths, or "downward," into the realm of primal religion? What has been the actual pattern of missionary success in the past? What developments are likely in the "one world" so recently created by modern communications?

VII
Christian Belief
and Interfaith Dialogue

Dialogue, or discussion, between people of different faiths takes place on various levels and in a variety of contexts. There is, first, discursive theological dialogue, concerned with the truth claims of the different religions. But this should always broaden out to include ways of life and forms of art and symbolism, and it should involve opportunities to observe or even participate in one another's religious life at its focal point of worship and contemplation. Here it may begin to pass into a second form of dialogue, the interior dialogue, practiced and reported by such Christian pioneers as the late Père H. le Saux (Swami Abhishiktananda) and Dom Bede Griffiths in India. And then, third, there is the more immediately practical dialogue concerned with common human problems and exemplified, for example, by the Buddhist-Christian-Hindu-Jewish-Muslim discussions at Colombo in 1974, whose report is entitled *Towards World Community: Resources and Responsibilities for Living Together.*

I shall be concerned here primarily with discursive dialogue, though with the understanding that this may pass naturally into the deeper interior dialogue, and also that a common concern about world community is a very proper part of the agenda of interreligious dialogue today, and one to which I shall return at the end of this chapter.

Discursive or theological dialogue, then, takes place

somewhere on or moving about within a spectrum which ranges between two opposite conceptions of its nature. At one extreme there is purely confessional dialogue, in which each partner witnesses to his own faith, convinced that this has absolute truth while his partner's has only relative truth. At the other extreme is truth-seeking dialogue, in which each is conscious that the transcendent Being is infinitely greater than his own limited vision of it, and in which the partners accordingly seek to share their visions in the hope that each may be helped toward a fuller awareness of the divine Reality before which they both stand. Dialogue sometimes takes place nearer to one pole and sometimes nearer to the other, but often varies in character as it proceeds, moving back and forth along the scale.

I

Let us look first at the confessional end of the dialogical spectrum. Here the Christian, in dialogue with people of other faiths, speaks from within his own conviction that God has entered decisively into human history in the person of Jesus Christ, the second Person of the holy Trinity incarnate, who has revealed the divine nature and purpose for man in a unique and unsurpassable way in comparison with which all other revelations must necessarily be secondary, in the sense of being incomplete, or imperfect, or preliminary, or in some other way vitally inferior to the Christian revelation.

This confessional attitude to other religions derives in recent theology from the massive dogmatic work of Karl Barth (particularly the relatively early Barth of *Church Dogmatics*, I/2) and the detailed application of this to the world religions by the great Dutch missionary scholar Hendrik Kraemer in his immensely influential book *The Christian Message in a Non-Christian World*, written for the World Missionary Conference at Tambaram, near

Madras, in 1938. So long as this stance was dominant within the World Council of Churches, as it was until the end of the general secretaryship of Dr. Visser 't Hooft in 1966, this great ecumenical vehicle refrained from inter-religious dialogue. Since then, however, dialogue has become the order of the day, and instead of a confessional rejection of dialogue we have now a confessional stance within dialogue. For those who adopt this stance, the Christian revelation is not one among several, but is the only true revelation of God. This has recently been articulated as follows by the distinguished missionary theologian, Bishop Lesslie Newbigin:

> A Christian who participates in dialogue with people of other faiths will do so on the basis of his faith. The presuppositions which shape his thinking will be those which he draws from the Gospel. This must be quite explicit. He cannot agree that the position of final authority can be taken by anything other than the Gospel—either by a philosophical system, or by mystical experience, or by the requirements of national and global unity. Confessing Christ—incarnate, crucified and risen—as the true light and the true life, he cannot accept any other's alleged authority as having right of way over this. He cannot regard the revelation given in Jesus as one of a type, or as requiring to be interpreted by means of categories based on other ways of understanding the totality of experience. Jesus is—for the believer—the source from whom his understanding of the totality of experience is drawn and therefore the criterion by which other ways of understanding are judged. ("The Basis, Purpose and Manner of Inter-Faith Dialogue," *Scottish Journal of Theology*, Vol. 30, No. 3, 1977, p. 255)

From this point of view the Christian, however personally open and charitable toward people of other faiths, is necessarily bearing witness, or confessing his faith, and he is bound to hope that his hearers will respond to the Word of God which reaches them through his words, and commit themselves to Christ as the way, the truth, and the life. Thus Bishop Newbigin says that the Christian's purpose in entering into dialogue with people of other faiths "can only be obedient witness to Jesus Christ. Any other purpose, any goal which subordinates the honor of Jesus Christ to some purpose derived from another source, is impossible for the Christian. To accept such another purpose would involve a denial of the total lordship of Jesus Christ. A Christian cannot try to evade the accusation that, for him, dialogue is part of his obedient witness to Jesus Christ" (p. 265). Here we see the confessional position adopted as an explicit stance within dialogue.

Needless to say, there is an equivalent confessional stance for the adherents of any other of the religions and ideologies. It is important to keep this fact in mind, because while from within a particular confessional circle of faith one has the impression of standing at the center of the world of meaning, with all other faiths dispersed around its periphery, from the point of view of global history it is evident that there are many different circles of faith, with the inhabitants of each living under the same impression of their own unique centrality. Let us, then, briefly take note of this plurality of centers by referring to Islam, as another Semitic faith; to advaitic Hinduism, as representing a very different kind of religion; and to Marxism, as a powerful secular rival to the traditional religions.

The confessing Muslim, in interreligious dialogue, will speak from within his own faith that Islam represents the latest and fullest revelation, taking up and completing the earlier revelations through Moses and the prophets down to and including Jesus. He will see much good in other religions, particularly in Judaism and Christianity as kindred religions of the Book; but it will be his firm conviction that Islam is the final revelation; and he will inevitably hope that in confessing his faith he may be the instrument of Allah in leading others to commit themselves to the living relationship to God which is Islam.

Again, the Hindu who adheres to the truth revealed in the Vedas and Upanishads as interpreted in the advaitic tradition will speak with people of other faiths from within his conviction that the absolute Reality is beyond all human categories, and that the worship of a personal God occurs on a lower and preliminary level of the religious life. He will see all religions as paths toward the final good of union with the Ultimate, but will see these paths as eventually converging upon the direct way revealed in Advaita Vedanta. Unlike the Christian and the Muslim, however, he will not feel obliged to try to press his own spiritual knowledge upon others, for he believes that they will accept it for themselves when they are ready for it—if not in this life, then in some future life.

Then there is the Marxist in dialogue with religious believers. Whether Marxism is to be accounted a religion is a matter of definition. Personally I prefer a definition of "religion" which involves an essential reference to the Transcendent and which consequently does not include Marxism. Nevertheless, Marxism borders on the religions in that it is a systematic interpretation of human existence which issues in a distinctive way of life; and as such it constitutes one of the most powerful options among the world's living religions and ideologies. And when a Marxist engages in dialogue with people of other faiths than his own he does so from within his conviction that Marxism teaches the truth about man and his history, including the truth that man's religions are projections of human hope, whose historic function has been to enable the exploited masses to bear their servitude patiently rather than rise up against their oppressors. And it must be his hope that through his proclamation of Marxist truth his hearers will be converted and enlisted among the forces of progress.

When these four come together in confessional dialogue, each must in the end be bearing witness to his own faith. But it may be that each is also of an open-minded and inquiring disposition, desirous of learning as well as of bearing witness. They will then come to know about one another's convictions and will be able to compare the different features of their respective belief systems. But still, insofar as they hold to the absolute truth of their own traditions, each will be basically concerned to try to bring the others to share his own faith.

For example, the Christian may enunciate what has traditionally been regarded as the central truth of his faith, namely that Jesus Christ was God the Son incarnate. The Muslim will respond that Jesus was indeed the greatest of the line of prophets before Muhammad himself; and he will acknowledge that Jesus was born of a virgin mother, as the scriptures say. But he will insist that it would be blasphemy to hold that he was actually and literally God, in the sense of being one of the three Persons of a divine Trinity. The Hindu will say that Jesus was indeed a divine incarnation, one of the series of avatars which continues down perhaps to Sri Ramakrishna and Mahatma Gandhi in the nineteenth and twentieth centuries. And the Marxist will say that since God is an illusion, it must be an illusion to think that Jesus was in any sense God incarnate. He was rather a great moral revolutionary whom the church has captured and used for its own counterrevolutionary purposes.

And so long as they all stand firmly within their own respective circles of faith, the dialogue will consist basically in the display and comparison of these incompatible beliefs.

However, interreligious dialogue undertaken just like that, as two (or more) people bearing mutual witness to their own faiths, each in the firm conviction that his is the final truth and in hope of converting the other, can only result either in conversion or in a hardening of differences—occasionally the former but more often the latter.

In order for dialogue to be mutually fruitful, lesser changes than total conversion must be possible and must be hoped for on both (or all) sides. In principle this is readily acknowledged by many contemporary Christian advocates of the confessional stance. Thus Bishop Newbigin says: "We are eager to receive from our partners what God has given them, to hear what God has shown them. In our meeting with men of other faiths we are learning to share in our common patrimony as human beings made by the one God in his own image" (p. 266). He also grants, and indeed affirms, that not only the non-Christian but also the Christian himself should be changed in the course of the dialogue. Indeed he says, "Much of his own 'Christianity' may have to be left behind in this meeting. Much of the intellectual construction, the piety, the practice in which our discipleship of Christ has been expressed may have to be called in question" (p. 268).

Here we approach the living heart of our problem, as it affects the Christian. For the question is, how serious and how radical can this possibility of change be in the Christian partner? Suppose that, in the experience of dialogue, *more* of "the intellectual construction . . . in which his discipleship of Christ has been expressed" is called in question than he anticipated? Are there then to be reserved areas of belief which must remain exempt from the possibility of change? May it indeed turn out that he was only playing at openness to change in his own understanding, but that in reality he stood throughout firmly upon a dogmatic conception of what his Christianity must be—a conception which simply corresponded to the traditional structure of Christian orthodoxy?

Let us pursue these questions a little further. In allowing for significant change in the Christian as a fruit of his dialogue with non-Christians it is customary to draw a very important distinction (suggested by that of Karl Barth) between, on the one hand, the historical phenomenon called Christianity, which is one of the religions of the world, and, on the other hand, personal discipleship and devotion to Jesus Christ. This implies an entirely proper and helpful distinction between Jesus—the actual Jesus who lived in Palestine in the first third of the first century, the reports and rumors of whose life and teaching have inspired millions ever since to try to live as his disciples—and the historical development of Christianity, the latter being recognized to be a human, and often all-too-human, affair. And the contemporary confessionalist often suggests that we should engage in dialogue, not primarily as adherents of historical Christianity but simply as disciples of Jesus.

This is, I think, a very fruitful approach. But where it will lead must depend to an important extent upon investigations concerning the historical Jesus, to whom it appeals, and of the ways in which the Christian interpretation of him has been formed over the centuries. The all-important question concerns the extent to which the man Jesus is to be understood in terms of the developed theology of the church. For the confessionalist it is usually an unquestioned assumption that belief in the doctrines of the incarnation and the Trinity are essentially involved in personal discipleship to Jesus. But it is precisely this assumption that has been directly questioned in many recent discussions of Christian origins and of the development of Christian thought, and that is today at the center of a considerable debate. To cite just one major evidence of this, in the 1976 Report of the Church of England's Doctrine Commission, the chairman, in his own essay, wrote that, in using traditional Christian language about Jesus as God's only Son, he is "using language in a very indirect, even poetic, way to express the central role of Jesus in giving form and life to our faith in God" (*Christian Believing,* p. 129); and concerning the doctrine of the Trinity he wrote: "I cannot with integrity say that I believe God to be one in three persons" (p. 126). If the Commission's then chairman, who is also Regius Professor of Divinity at Oxford, can take this view—a view, it should be added, with which some of his colleagues agreed but with which others strongly disagreed—we are clearly in a period of theological reflection in which these doctrines which were once accepted largely without question have now become matters of open debate. And the publication in 1977 of the book *The Myth of God Incarnate* by seven British theologians has opened this debate to a larger public. We can all see at least the possibility that the doctrines of the incarnation and the Trinity may turn out to be part of the "intellectual construction" which has to be left behind when the disciple of Jesus discards the cultural packaging in which Western Christianity has wrapped the gospel.

II

To indicate how this has come about I would remind you that fifty years ago it was widely assumed in Christian circles that Jesus lived his life in the awareness of being God the Son incarnate. It was assumed in much Christian preaching that Jesus knew himself to be divine; that he walked the earth with conscious divine authority, knowledge, and power; and that he taught his own unique divine status in such sayings as "I and my Father are one," "No man cometh unto the Father but by me"; "He that hath seen me hath seen the Father." But that position has become very difficult to sustain in the light of continuing biblical study. It is now widely accepted that the great Christological sayings of the Fourth Gospel express the theology of the church—or at least of an important part of the church—toward the end of the first century; that it is uncertain whether the historical Jesus accepted the designation of Messiah, or Christ; that the meaning of the phrase which he undoubtedly did use of himself, namely, "Son of Man," is still unclear; and that it cannot be established historically that Jesus thought of himself as more than that as which he seems to have been presented in the earliest Christian preaching, namely: "Jesus of Nazareth, a man attested to you by God with mighty works and wonders and signs which God did through him in your midst" (Acts 2: 22). It is accordingly widely acknowledged that if Jesus was indeed God the Son incarnate, he did not know this during his earthly life. Indeed, because of the implausibility of maintaining the divine self-consciousness of the historical Jesus, many are today attracted by the new theory that it was in his resurrection that Jesus either became, or became conscious of being, the Son of God or God the Son.

Such speculations have moved a long way from the original proposition that Jesus of Nazareth presented himself as God the Son living a human life. A further move which many today feel constrained to take acknowledges that the idea of divine incarnation is a poetic or symbolic or mythological way of speaking of God's powerful presence to a faithful human being and through him to others. Whether such a development of Christian understanding is right or wrong is not a matter to be quickly or easily settled, and the current renewed phase of intense Christological discussion may well have to continue for a long time. My own view is that the Christian mind will almost inevitably come to see the doctrine of the incarnation, and the doctrine of the Trinity which grew out of it, in a new way, no longer as precise metaphysical truths but as imaginative constructions giving expression—in the religious and philosophical language of the ancient world—to the Christian's devotion to Jesus as the one who has made the heavenly Father real to him. Or at any rate, I would suggest that this is the kind of development which the more intellectual part of the Christian mind (appropriately, in the human brain, the left hemisphere!) is likely to undergo, while its more emotional other half perhaps continues to use the traditional language of Christian mythology without raising troublesome questions about its meaning. But there may be sufficient overall development for the Christian position in interfaith dialogue to change in character. It may no longer be necessary to insist, however gently, upon the uniqueness and superiority of Christianity; and it may be possible to recognize the separate validity of the other great world religions, and both to learn from them and enable them to learn from the Christian tradition.

This development is continuous with some three centuries of internal change in response to the challenges of modern science and philosophy. Christianity is the first of the ancient world faiths to have attained—however unevenly and falteringly—to a new self-understanding in the light of the scientific revolution; and its gift to the other great religious traditions can now be its own experience of modernization, communicated both in interfaith dialogue and in other ways. This is the role of "critical catalyst" of which Hans Küng has recently written (*On Being a Christian*, pp. 100f.). The Christian responsibility and opportunity are both alike great. For it is for the most part Christian agencies—such as the World Council of Churches' Programme on Dialogue with People of Living Faiths and Ideologies—that are today most actively promoting interreligious dialogue; so that the ethos of the Christian ecumenical movement tends at the same time to set the tone for the wider world ecumenical dialogue.

If it is to fulfill its special role during this new period of religious history, Christianity must, I believe, move emphatically from the confessional to the truth-seeking stance in dialogue. And indeed to a great extent this has already happened, as is shown by the Guidelines for Inter-Religious Dialogue formulated in 1972 by Dr. Stanley Samartha of the World Council of Churches. In this document it is first affirmed: "The basis of interreligious dialogue is the commitment of all partners to their respective faiths and their openness to the insights of the others. The integrity of particular religions must be recognised." This statement acknowledges the degree of validity within the confessional stance, but places it within the context of religious pluralism. It is then said that the objective of dialogue is not a superficial consensus or a dilution of convictions, but "it must lead to the enrichment of all in the discovery of new dimensions of Truth." Finally, after a series of valuable recommendations about the need to go beyond purely intellectual discussion and even to participate in one another's worship, and also to be prepared to take concrete action together for world peace, the document concludes with a statement of the truth-seeking ideal for dialogue: "Inter-religious dialogue should also stress the need to study fundamental questions in the religious dimension of life Religions are man's responses to the mystery of existence and quests for meaning in the midst of confusion. World religious organisations should support the long-range study of the deeper questions which today ought to be taken up not just separately by individuals of each religion, but also together in the larger interests of mankind." ("The Progress and Promise of Inter-Religious Dialogues," *Journal of Ecumenical Studies*, 1972, pp. 473f.) This seems to me to be the right method and approach.

III

The main impact, in response to which Christianity has undergone the transformations of the last three centuries, is of course that of modern science; and we must ask how the other world religions are likely to respond to the same impact, coming to them from the West in a more powerful form as the impact of an already between Koranic fundamentalists and liberals paralleling, but perhaps deeper and more bitter than, that between Christian fundamentalists and liberals. We must hope that the experience of interfaith dialogue will be helpful to Islam during this difficult period of its history.

IV

Finally, let us turn from the impact of science and technology to the moral and social criticisms and suggestions which the world's faiths may have to offer one another as the interactions between them develop. We can at this point resume the Christian-Muslim-Hindu-Marxist dialogue which we began earlier. This is of course only a segment of the larger and more complex network of world dialogue; and even within this limited segment I am only going to pick out a single question from among the many that will be directed to each of the partners to the dialogue. But this will perhaps serve to illustrate the kind of mutual questioning that is to be expected.

One of the questions put to Hindu India in the dialogue of faiths will concern the caste system—officially rejected in India since 1949 but still in practice persisting in many ways—according to which each individual is born into a particular caste and subcaste which determines his or her occupation, social circle, choice of marriage partner, and spiritual status; and leaving outside the system, with no social or spiritual status at all, the outcastes or untouchables, whom Mahatma Gandhi renamed Harijans, children of God. Is not this a fundamentally unjust system, denying the basic concept of the equality of all mankind? The answer can, surely, only be that this is so. The caste system stands under the same condemnation as feudal social hierarchies, the class structure in many modern Western societies, and the assumption of white superiority and black and brown inferiority which is still so evident among most white Christian populations. But we must remember that in condemning distinctions of caste, class, and color we are speaking from the point of view of a modern liberal concept of human equality which has only recently come to widespread consciousness. If we ask where this immensely important concept has come from, the answer would seem to be that the abstract idea is present in all the major religious traditions, but that its activation as a political force in the world, first in Europe and the United States and then increasingly throughout the world, has resulted from the general undermining of hierarchical authority as a modern has superseded a medieval mentality. India has not yet completed this transition from the medieval to the modern world, and is still in its struggle to throw off the ancient caste system. It must be added that conservative Hinduism continues to be the last stronghold of caste, and that the influence of Christianity, Marxism, and Islam upon Hinduism must be toward the final purging of the blight of caste from the life of India.

One of the questions put to Islam in the multilateral dialogue of faiths will concern the status of women in Muslim societies. The issue here is partly polygamy and partly the traditional subordination of women within patriarchal societies. The respective merits of monogamy and polygamy deserve to be debated in the light of the growing knowledge of human nature offered by psychology and sociology. But polygamy must also be seen in relation to the different stages of social history. Why is it that polygamy was practiced in the societies reflected both in the Koran and in the earlier strata of the Old Testament, but has subsequently died out in Jewish society and is today dying out in Arab societies? It may well be that the liberation of women, which naturally excludes polygamy, is part of a general process of liberation as humanity "comes of age" in the modern world.

But the challenge faces Islam to come to terms with this new outlook, including its effect in liberating women.

One of the major questions put to the Marxists and Maoists in their dialogue with the religions will concern individual human freedom. The religions will have increasingly to recognize a considerable element of truth in the Marxist analysis of the economic dynamics of human society, and a common aim with Marxism in the ideal of a classless society in which men no longer exploit one another. Indeed the moral basis for the criticism both of the Hindu caste system and of polygamy and the traditional subordination of women is most clearly articulated in Marxism. For Marxism embodies in its pure form the mentality produced by the scientific revolution. Marxism is modernity without religion, in contrast to much of contemporary Christianity, which is modernity in a religious form. But the Marxist societies have to face the question whether, in their opposition to capitalist-Christian civilization, they have not themselves become hierarchical and authoritarian, thus negating the concept of human liberation on which they are based. For there are clearly as many features of Marxist as of Christian, Muslim, and Hindu societies which contradict the modern ideal of human equality and freedom.

What questions will the other partners in the ecumenical dialogue put to Christianity? We have seen that the most distinctive feature of the societies of Europe, North America, and Australasia has been that they belong to the modern world. They look across the great gulf of the scientific and technological revolutions to their own medieval past and to the lingering medieval present of many other parts of the world. For Christendom was the civilization within which the transformation of medieval into modern man first took place and through whose influence it is therefore taking place elsewhere. This is Christianity's unique historical role. If we relate the contingencies of history to an overarching divine purpose of creating children of God out of human animals, we can say that it has been Christianity's special vocation to give birth to the modern mentality. But this calling also has its perils and temptations. In being the first science-based culture, Christendom is also the first culture to experience the domination, possibly leading to the destruction, of human life by its own technology. For technology has created the self-consuming consumer society, with its selfish assumption of a continually rising standard of living. This assumption—together with the population explosion made possible by medical technology—is rapidly exhausting the earth's basic mineral and energy resources and creating the prospect of ecological disaster, perhaps in the early decades of the next century. Western civilization may thus be in process of strangling itself by its own unbridled lust for ever greater wealth and luxury; or may indeed destroy itself abruptly in a massive thermonuclear exchange in which the deeply ingrained Western habit of violence puts the marvels of modern technology to suicidal use. Christianity has so far offered no effective resistance to this trend, but is on the contrary deeply implicated in the self-destructive lifestyle and violent tradition of modern Western man. The question is now whether Christian civilization, having become the first bearer of the modern scientific spirit, can avoid being so dominated and corrupted by it that it leads the whole world to destruction.

I am not going to end with any ringing statement of confidence that mankind will succeed in overcoming its immense problems—with the Islamic, Hindu, and Buddhist worlds making their transition from a medieval to a modern mentality without succumbing to the dangers so evident in the West; with the Marxist and Maoist civilizations developing their own forms of personal freedom and creativity; and with the Christian West learning nonviolence from the profoundly peaceful tradition of Buddhism, and learning a certain detachment from material possessions from traditional Hindu wisdom. I do not profess to know whether any of these things will happen. But what can be said with assurance is that each of the great streams of faith within which human life is lived can learn from the others; and that any hope for the future lies largely in the world ecumenical dialogue which is taking place in so many ways and at so many levels.

probably circulated in different branches of his school, for of quotations from the Master by the two most important of the early Confucians, Mencius and Hsün-tzu, most of the former's and all of the latter's are missing from the *Analects*. The *Analects* itself shows signs of accretion; in particular the last five chapters (chs. 16–20) differ considerably from the rest. However, given a book homogeneous in thought, marked by a strong and individual mind, and with inadequate criteria at our disposal for distinguishing the voice of the original teacher (very much as with the Gospel sayings of Jesus), it is convenient to accept it as the record of the earliest stage of Confucianism without asking how much of it is in the actual words of the founder.

The Confucius of the *Analects* is a teacher, surrounded by a circle of disciples, who vainly aspires to the high office which would enable him to reform government; he sets a precedent which will be followed by philosophers for the next three centuries by travelling with his disciples from state to state seeking a ruler who will listen to him. He wins audiences from Duke Ling of Wei (534–493 B.C.), Duke Ching of Ch'i (547–490 B.C.), and in his own state of Lu Dukes Ting (509–495 B.C.) and Ai (494–468 B.C.). It may be a mistake to think of him as finding his message first and attracting disciples afterwards. His thought and his sense of mission are of a kind which might develop naturally from the experience of an ordinary teacher of the *Songs, Documents*, ceremony, and music of Chou, distinguished at first only in that his disciples learn from him, as from an inspiring schoolmaster, much more than is on the curriculum. The *Tso Commentary* records that in 518 B.C. Meng Hsi-tzu of Lu, humiliated by his own ignorance of ritual, sent his two sons to Confucius, purely to study ceremony.

Ceremony and music

Let us start with Confucius as he sees himself, the preserver and restorer of a declining culture, who would not presume to invent anything.

"In transmitting but not originating, trusting in and loving the ancient, I would venture to compare myself to our old P'eng." (*Analects* 7/1)

In studying the *Documents* and *Songs* of early Chou, and the ceremonies and music, Confucius recognises the importance of thinking, but is inclined to put the stress rather on learning.

"To learn without thinking is stultifying, to think without learning is dangerous." (2/15)

"I used to go without food all day, without sleep all night, to think. No use, better to learn." (15/31)

"My disciples, why does none of you learn the *Songs*? The *Songs* may be used to stir imagination, to become observant, to get people together, to complain, at home in serving your father and abroad in serving your lord; and you will remember many names of birds, animals, plants and trees." (17/9)

This may seem an unpromising beginning to a philosophical tradition, but let us continue. The institutions which for Confucius are central to Chou culture are its ceremony and its music. The word *li* 禮 'ceremony' embraces all rites, custom, manners, conventions, from the sacrifices to ancestors down to the detail of social etiquette. *Li* in social intercourse corresponds to a considerable extent with Western conceptions of good manners; the Confucian gentleman moves with an effortless grace within the framework of fixed convention, informing every action with consideration and respect for the other person. *Yüeh* 樂 ('music'), which embraces dance, is primarily the music and dance of sacred rites; correspondingly, ceremony is continuous with music in being conducted with style like an artistic performance. What above all distinguishes *li* from Western conceptions of good manners is that for Confucius it has everywhere the efficacy of sacred rite, an efficacy in transforming human relations which is independent of the powers to which explicitly religious rituals are addressed.

The enormous importance which Confucius ascribes to ceremony by no means implies that he identifies the ritual with the moral. He has a different word, *yi* 義 (related to another *yi* 宜 'fitting'), for the right, which is conceived as the conduct fitting to one's role or status, for example as father or son, ruler or minister.

"It is the right which the gentleman deems the substance, it is through ceremony that he performs it, through humility that he expresses it, through being trustworthy that he perfects it, the gentleman!" (15/18)

"If those above love ceremony, none of the people will presume to be irreverent; if they love the right, none will presume to disobey; if they love trustworthiness, none will presume to be insincere." (13/4)

The effect of ceremonial forms in the social hierarchy is, as this last passage implies, that instead of actions merely being fitted to each other as right (the people *obeying* the ruler) attitudes become harmonious (the people *revering* the ruler).

"The disciple Yu-tzu said 'In the employment of ceremony it is harmony which is most to be valued. In the Way of the former kings it is this which is most beautiful, follow it in small things and great. Where things are not on course, if you harmonise by the knowledge of harmony without regulating it by ceremony, they still cannot be put on course." (1/12)

Music no doubt also inspires this harmony, although Confucius never theorises about its overwhelming effect on himself.

"The Master while in Ch'i heard the Shao, and for three months did not notice the taste of meat. He said 'I did not conceive that making music had reached such heights.'" (7/14)

Chapter 10 of the Analects records detailed observations of the Master's own ceremonial performance.

"When summoned by his lord to serve as usher, his expression was serious, his step brisk. When with clasped hands he bowed to his colleagues on left and right, his robes moved evenly in front and behind. His hurrying advance was a glide. When the guest withdrew he would invariably announce 'The guest no longer looks back.'" (10/2)

Although there are later ritualist texts which prescribe such details, Confucius himself never lays down rules about them. It may be presumed that his disciples noted points in the performance of the supreme artist in ceremony of which he would perhaps not himself be conscious, as refinements of a personal style from which one could learn without necessarily imitating him. There are items in the series in which his good manners plainly have nothing to do with prescribed forms.

"The stable caught fire. On returning from court the Master said 'Is anyone hurt?'. He did not ask about the horses." (10/11)

The past to which Confucius looks back is not the beginning of things; there is no cosmogonic myth in pre-Han literature, merely a blank of pre-history before the first Emperors, who for Confucius are the pre-dynastic sages Yao and Shun. Although interested in the institutions of all the Three Dynasties which followed he draws primarily on the last, the Chou, the one of which the tradition is not yet extinct. Indeed he sees history down to the Chou not as regress but as progress.

"Chou had the two earlier dynasties as examples to it. How glorious is its culture! I follow Chou." (3/14)

In spite of this fidelity to Chou he sees the rebuilding of contemporary culture as a process of selecting and evaluating past and present models.

"The Master called the Shao music both perfectly beautiful and perfectly good. He called the Wu music perfectly beautiful but not perfectly good." (3/25)

"Lin Fang asked about the basic in ceremony. The Master said 'An

excellent question! In ceremony prefer the thrifty to the extravagant, in mourning put grief before meticulousness.'" (3/4)

Elsewhere we see him applying the former of these critical principles to a traditional observance.

"To wear a hempen cap is the ceremony, but the black silk cap of today is thriftier, so I follow the majority. To prostrate oneself before ascending the steps is the ceremony, but today people prostrate themselves at the top, which is lax; even at the cost of diverging from the majority I do it before ascending." (9/3)

Government as ceremony

A pair of concepts first prominent in the Analects is Tao 道 'the Way' and te 德 'Potency'. In this text Tao is used only of the proper course of human conduct and of the organisation of government, which is the Way of 'antiquity', of 'the former kings', of 'the gentleman', of 'the good man' and of 'Wen and Wu' the founders of Chou, or else of what someone teaches as the Way ('my Way', and 'our master's Way'). Confucius does not use it, as Confucians as well as Taoists soon came to do, of the course of the natural world outside man. Te, which has often been translated as 'virtue' (to be understood as in 'The virtue of cyanide is to poison' rather than in 'Virtue is its own reward'), had been traditionally used of the power, whether benign or baleful, to move others without exerting physical force. Confucius uses it in this sense of the charisma of Chou which won it universal allegiance, but moralises and widens the concept, so that it becomes the capacity to act according to and bring others to the Way.

The two concepts are interdependent, as later in Lao-tzu (also entitled Tao te ching 'Classic of the Way and of Potency'): a person's te is his potentiality to act according to the Tao.

"One not persistent in maintaining Potency, not sincere in his trust in the Way, how can you tell whether he is there or he isn't?" (19/2)

"Be intent on the Way, be grounded in Potency, rely on nobility, take recreation in the arts." (7/6)

An extremely remarkable feature of Confucius' thought is his conviction that all government can be reduced to ceremony. In a state which has the Way the ruler wins the reverent submission of all by ceremony alone without the need of force, through the Potency which emanates from his person. In an age when government was detaching itself more and more from the ritual functions of kings this indeed looks like a reversion to an obsolete past of primitive magic (although we shall later be re-examining this point in the light of Fingarette's observations): as Schwartz notices, the early Chou *Documents* already give great weight to penal law.[2]

"Are you capable of ruling the state by ceremony and deference? Then what difficulties will you have? If you are incapable of ruling the state by ceremony and deference, what have you to do with ceremony?" (4/13)

"If you guide them by government, hold them even by punishment, the people will elude you and have no shame. If you guide them by Potency, hold them even by ceremony, the people will both have shame and draw near you." (2/3)

Confucius accepts law as belonging to the apparatus of government,[3] but measures success in ruling by how little it is necessary to apply it.

"In hearing litigation I am no different from others, but the point is surely to bring it about that there is no litigation!" (12/13)

"Chi-k'ang-tzu asked Confucius about government: 'What if we were to execute those who have not the Way to get nearer to those who have it?'

'When you engage in government,' Confucius answered, 'what need have you for executions? If you desire to be good the people will be good. The gentleman's Potency is the wind, the small man's Potency is the grass. The grass in the wind from above is sure to bend.'" (12/19)

Although Confucius protests at excessive taxation and recognises the need to enrich the people before expecting them to respond to teaching,[4] he sees the radical cure of social ills, not indeed in simply returning to Chou institutions, but in arranging the ideal court ceremonial by a critical selection from the rituals of the Three Dynasties, Hsia, Yin or Shang, and Chou.

"Yen Yüan asked about ruling a state. The Master said 'Put into effect the calendar of Hsia, ride the carriage of Yin, wear the cap of Chou. For music, the Shao and Wu. Banish the airs of Cheng and keep glib people at a distance. The airs of Cheng are wanton, glib people are dangerous.'" (15/11)

Ideally the ruler should not have to do anything at all, simply trust to the Potency which radiates from him. Confucius once even uses the term *wu wei* 無為 'doing nothing' later to become characteristic of Taoism.

"One who put in order by doing nothing, would not that be Shun? What is there that he did? Just assumed a respectful posture and faced south." (15/5)

"One who engages in government by Potency may be compared to the North Star; it occupies its place and all the stars pay homage to it." (2/1)

This can hardly be intended as practical politics, but there is no question of his confidence in Potency as a universal civilizing influence.

"The Master wished to live among the barbarian Nine Tribes. Someone said 'They're uncouth, what about that?' He said 'If a gentleman lived among them what uncouthness would there be?'" (9/14)

This is not quite the faith in the universal influence of the good man which Mencius was later to support by his doctrine of the goodness of human nature. It is rather a faith in the power of trained manners, customs, and rituals to harmonise attitudes and open the inferior to the influence of the superior. His single reference to human nature emphasises not man's goodness but his malleability.

"The Master said 'By nature we are near to each other, by habituation we diverge.' The Master said 'Only the highest wisdom and lowest folly do not shift.'" (17/2)

Heaven and the spirits

When in the 17th and 18th centuries Confucius first attracted attention in the West many saw him as a rationalist sceptical of the existence of supernatural beings. To Westerners preoccupied with the emerging conflict between reason and religion this seemed the obvious interpretation. It took some time to appreciate that, except for the Mohists, no one in ancient China much cared whether consciousness survives death or whether Heaven is a personal God or impersonal principle, issues of overwhelming importance to Jesuits and *philosophes*. The attitude of Confucius is that we should not be diverted from human affairs by matters which do not concern us. There is no reason to question that he recognises the sacrifices to Heaven, mountain and river gods, and ghosts of ancestors, as the greatest of ceremonies, harmonising not only man with man but man with cosmos. But for him the value of ceremony is in the harmony itself and does not depend on anything outside. He is not interested in how the sacrifices relate us to cosmos; our business is with man, and to speculate about the realm of the numinous is idle curiosity. It is not so much that he is a sceptic as that he does not care whether you are a sceptic or not.

"The Master did not talk about marvels, feats of strength, irregularities, gods." (7/21)

Chi-lu asked about serving the ghosts and gods. The Master said, 'Until you can serve men how can you serve the ghosts?'

'Permit me to ask about death.'

'Until you know about life how can you know about death?' (11/12)

"Fan Ch'ih asked about wisdom. The Master said 'To work at doing right for the people, and to be reverent to the ghosts and gods but keep them at a distance, may be called wisdom." (6/22)

"He sacrificed as though they were present, sacrificed to gods as though the gods were present. The Master said 'Unless I involve myself in the sacrifice it is as though I did not sacrifice." (3/12)

A story in a Han anthology of largely pre-Han material, unlikely to be genuine but very typically Confucian, has the Master judging the propriety of questions about the spirits entirely by the consequences for human behaviour.

"Tzu-kung asked Confucius whether the dead have knowledge or not. Confucius said: 'If I preferred to say that they do have knowledge, I am afraid that filial sons and obedient grandsons would hinder life to send off the dead. If I preferred to say that they do not, I am afraid that unfilial offspring would abandon the dead without burial. If you wish to know whether the dead have knowledge or not, delaying until death to know it for yourself you still won't be too late.'"5

The shift of attention to the human realm, and refusal to speculate outside its range, became general throughout the age of the philosophers. The question whether "the dead have knowledge" is raised occasionally, but in terms of whether ghosts can harm the living, not of personal survival; the only kind of immortality welcomed, when the prospect of it was conceived in the 3rd century B.C., is the prolongation of life by elixirs, not survival as a ghost. Some, including the Confucian Hsün-tzu, take it for granted that consciousness ends at death. Otherwise, except by the Mohists, who do argue at length that the dead are conscious, the issue is left open and treated as a theme for wit rather than serious argument. Thus in a story which turns up in the 3rd century B.C. a king of Ch'u is about to sacrifice two prisoners of war in order to smear his battle drums with their blood; they escape this fate by arguing

"If the dead lack knowledge, it will be pointless to use us to smear the drums; if they do have knowledge, when you are about to go into battle we shall stop the drums sounding."6

In 265 B.C., according to another story, Queen Hsüan of Ch'in on her deathbed commanded that her lover be buried alive with her, but was similarly dissuaded.

"Do you think that the dead have knowledge?'

'They do not,' said the Queen.

'If Your Majesty's divine intelligence plainly knows that the dead lack knowledge, why uselessly bury the man you loved in life beside an unknowing corpse? But if the dead do have knowledge, his late Majesty's wrath has been mounting for a long time.'"7

Only the Mohists take the issue wholly seriously. Besides arguing in detail that ghosts and gods exist and are conscious they point out as contradicting himself a Confucian who maintains both that "Ghosts and gods do not exist" and that "The gentleman must learn the sacrificial ceremonies."8

Whether Heaven is a personal or impersonal power is another issue on which no one argues except the Mohists, who accuse the Confucians of holding that "Heaven is unseeing and the ghosts are not daimonic"9, that is, they lack the daimonic insight which uncovers secret wrongdoing. It is in any case a question of degree, for even such as Hsün-tzu, for whom Heaven is highly impersonal, have no other paradigm than a human ruler and fall into personifying imagery. In the case of Confucius, his reticence allows us to see only that he tends to personify when pondering with awe and humility whether Heaven is on the side of his mission. It is a question he asks himself especially when in danger on his travels.

"Heaven generated the Potency in me, what can Huan T'ui do to me?" (7/23)

"When imprisoned in K'uang the Master said 'Since King Wen died has not the culture come to reside in me? If Heaven is about to abandon this culture, those who die afterwards will not get to share in it; if Heaven has not yet abandoned this culture, what can the men of K'uang do to me?" (9/5)

"The Master said 'There's no one, is there, who recognises me.' Tzu-kung said 'Why is it that no one recognises you?' The Master said 'I neither resent Heaven nor blame man; in learning about the lower I have fathomed the higher. The one who recognises me, wouldn't it be Heaven?'" (14/35)

Of the death of his favourite disciple, in whom he put his greatest hopes, we read

"When Yen Yüan died the Master said 'Alas, Heaven has abandoned me, Heaven has abandoned me." (11/9)

Confucius may be seen to fluctuate between a faith that Heaven will protect his mission and despair that Heaven has abandoned him. He struggles to understand 'destiny' (ming, literally 'decree', what Heaven has decreed). The reconciliation which he calls "knowing destiny" and claims to have attained10 at the age of 50 is a calm recognition that personal fortune and the rise and fall of good government are ultimately beyond man's control, and that to be at peace it is enough to have done one's best. When a disciple is endangered by a certain Kung-po Liao Confucius says

"The Way being about to prevail is destiny; the Way being about to fall to ruin is destiny. What can Kung-po Liao do about destiny?" (14/36)

"Ssu-ma Niu was worried that 'All other men have brothers, I have none.' Tzu-hsia said 'I have heard that death and life are destined, and riches and honours depend on Heaven. If the gentleman is reverent and without failings, and deals with others respectfully and with ceremony, everyone within the four seas will be a brother to him. What misfortune is it to the gentleman to have no brothers?'" (12/5)

It appears from the *Tso Commentary* that court historiographers, diviners, physicians and musicmasters already had a cosmology in which the course of the heavenly bodies was called the 'Way of Heaven'. To co-ordinate the Way of human custom and its seasonal festivals with the cycles of Heaven in a universal Way seems in retrospect an obvious step, and it was later to be made. But there is only one reference to the Way of Heaven in the *Analects*:

"What the Master has to say about human nature and the Way of Heaven we cannot get to hear." (5/13)

There is however one passage which implies a fundamental unity of life in Heaven and man. It suggests that with the perfect ritualisation of life we would understand our place in community and cosmos without the need of words, a thought which seems to anticipate Taoism.

"The Master said 'I should like to do without speech'. Tzu-kung said 'If you do not speak what message will your disciples have from you?', he said. 'Does Heaven speak?' 'The four seasons .proceed by it, the hundred things are generated by it. Does Heaven speak?" (17/19)

But the Way is mentioned explicitly only as the proper course of human conduct and government. Indeed he thinks of it as itself widened by the broadening of human culture.

"Man is able to enlarge the Way, it is not that the Way enlarges man." (15/29)

The thread which unifies morality

Until very recently most Western readers of Confucius tried to detach his moral thinking from its bedding in ceremony, which they discarded if not as dross then at any rate as significant only within Chinese society. The

major Confucian virtue *jen* 仁, commonly translated 'benevolence', an unselfish concern for the welfare of others, can indeed from Mencius onwards be understood in detachment from ceremony. But the translation 'benevolence' is not appropriate to the *Analects* itself, where Confucius is forming a new concept by adapting an old word to his own insights. *Jen* had been the stative verb corresponding to the noun *jen* 人 which the aristocratic clans of Chou used to distinguish themselves from the common people. Thus in two of the *Songs* a lady admires a man riding out to hunt as "handsome and martial", "handsome and strong", "handsome and *jen* (noble, lordly)". By the time of Confucius the noun *jen* was widening to the ordinary word for a human being. But throughout the history of Imperial China there was some hesitation in applying the noun to include barbarians, although it was always understood (as already by Confucius) that they are civilizable by the adoption of Chinese customs; genetically they are *jen*, but until civilized they tend to be classed rather with the beasts and birds. The noble, civilized, fully human, pride themselves on their manners and conventions, but above all on the virtues which give these meaning and which distinguish themselves from the boors and savages who do not know how to behave. The stative verb *jen*, as it was inherited by Confucius, covers like English 'noble' the whole range of superior qualities distinctive of the man of breeding. Granted that it is coming to mean 'human, humane' rather than 'noble', it may be convenient to stay with 'noble' as the *ad hoc* equivalent in the present chapter; being nearer to the older meaning, it suggests the sort of concept which Confucius is narrowing in the direction of benevolence. In any case he finds human qualities at their full flower only in the *chün-tzu* 君子 ('lord's son'), a word with very much the same social and moral range as English 'gentleman'. Its opposite is *hsiao-jen* 小人 'small man', 'vulgar man'.

Confucius more than once joins the stative verb with the noun, for example

"A noble who is ignoble (= a human who is inhuman), what has he to do with ceremony? A noble who is ignoble, what has he to do with music?" (3/3)

At the source of the varied qualities which distinguish the noble is a disinterested concern for the other person.

"Chung-kung asked about being noble (= human). The Master said 'Behave abroad as though welcoming an important guest, employ the people as though conducting an important sacrifice. What you do not